A Hungry Ghost
Surrenders His Tackle Box

Also by Maj Ragain

Poetry Books
Twist The Axe (2001)
Burley One Dark Sucker Fired (1998)
Fresh Oil, Loose Gravel (1996)
The Olney Dreadnot Book (1979)

Poetry Chapbooks
Vision to Verse/Verse to Vision (2004)
A Little Bastard Book for Buddha (1987)
Gail Ray's Drowning in Olney Poem (1987)
Father Sky (1984)
Northfield Thistledown Making Book (1981)
7 Poems (1980)
Jimmie The Vincennes Flyer (1977)

A Hungry Ghost Surrenders His Tackle Box

Maj Ragain

PAVEMENT SAW PRESS
OHIO

Editor : David Baratier
Associate Editor: Sean Karns
Front Cover & Interior Art:: Larry Marcell
Back Cover Photo: Jim Lang
Duck Logo: Joe Napora

Acknowledgments

The author wants to thank the editors of the following publications in which these poems first appeared: Artful Dodge, Angle: A Journal of Arts & Culture, Black Dirt, Cleveland Free Times, Pudding Magazine, Solo Flyer, Split Crimes, Split/Whiskey, The Heartlands Today, The New Kent Quarterly, The Time of Your Life, Worc's Aloud/Allowed.

And the following books: Art Crimes: The Sea of Forgetfulness, American Zen: A Gathering Of Poets, Carry On, Jawbone Book, Little Albert, Ornamental Iron, September 11, 2001/American Writers Respond, Sword & Shield, The Secret Life of a Deranged Poet, Broadside The Writer's Forum Reading Series, Vision to Verse/Verse to Vision, Working Hard for the Money.

Pavement Saw Press
PO Box 6291
Columbus, OH 43206
pavementsaw.org

Ohio Arts Council
A STATE AGENCY
THAT SUPPORTS PUBLIC
PROGRAMS IN THE ARTS

Products are available through the publisher or through:
SPD / 1341 Seventh St. / Berkeley, CA 94710 / 800.869.7553

CONTENTS

A LIST OF THINGS TO DO AROUND THE HOUSE THIS WINTER

Find my own way to belong to this world.
Drown in what I do everyday.
Befriend old grief, then kill it.
Pick the lock on my rib cage and leave it open.
Swallow hard and piss beautiful rust.
Make my bed with the hopeful.
Give up my breath to the moon, to the river,
to the men who sleep in their clothes,
to the women who comb their belly hair
and mark the trail home.
Learn to cut stone with my tongue.
Learn to do my own joy down to the bone.
Become the wild sweet freedom for which I yearn.
Seek out the homely mother of beautiful blood
who dances with the cold half moon.
Remember not to leave this world without ceremony.
Remember to look toward the sun after it is gone,
to cry out when there is no one to listen.

THANKING THE OAK HEART

My friend Jon Randall built me
a dinner table, a three inch slab of Hiram
century Oak steadied by four
legs, each a foot high, cut from
a barn beam. A cross section
of its seasons is chain sawed
open, ring by ring, the narrow
band of drought, the wide pulse
of a green year. A dark crack
tracks across the whorl,
that nebula held by its own center.
The table is the size of a monk's snowsled,
a knight's shield, a child's coffin,
a skateboard for a big-butted Buddha.

When the waters receded,
after the valleys were gouged from rock,
the leviathans, great legless beasts,
found themselves wallowing in the ebb tide.
In the last sounding, they staggered upright,
bone trunk hair reaching through the new earth,
holding, scale drying into bark.

I take my supper sitting on the floor.
The table is level with my heart.
I make a small blessing on it with my knuckles.

Old Oak heart, dark with deep,
we sit down with you.

The Body is a Cognitive Map

*The enlightenment of the wave is to
understand that it is water.*

—Thich Nhat Hanh

Doctor Verdena, every time the pneumonia returns,
and a little more of me wears away against the stone,
the brighter my soul flares, its carnival lights
strung across the boney mast of my shoulders.
The body is a temporary shelter, not my real home.
I don't want to become too accustomed
to things down here below,
the quick text of skin, the scarlet banner of appetite,
the consolations of children, work and dreams.
Conditions come together to give shape to the wave, the body.
When those conditions change, the form is altered.
This morning, all around me, the sea shines.
The sky opens into ocean.
I am turning away from shore, toward water.

THE PINE TREE HEAVY WITH SNOW SHRUGS

Tonight the automatic teller machine,
Society bank drive through, ate my deposit,
swallowed my magnetic strip braille card
and would not spit it back.
Three cars lined up behind me,
headlights at the base of my skull.
I cursed and drove away,
what I have always done.
The December mortgage check bounced
down Summit street.

The Chinese algebra of money,
tongue tied machine, my name
and numbers tattooed on the pale screen.
The yellow lines divide my day.
The traffic lights bark green and red.
No left turn here as long as I live.

The western sky was herringboned
pink, split salmon orange.
Meg, my small daughter, belted and bolted
to her seat, pointed.
Look, it's beautiful.

There is another life inside this one.

A drunken monk carves
a mountain landscape
into his thigh.
A childless woman, on her knees, sings
to a river's spring floodtide.
A blind man builds a longboat in his midnight basement.
A boy sleeps on the soft dirt of his father's grave.

Find that world.

Tell me the rest of it.

LITTLE POEMS OF YEARNING

When you leave someone you love,
you walk backwards.

In my dream, I kiss everyone
in the room, on the mouth.

Like a monk with scissors,
I must learn to make holes
in my habits.

I wish I had been sent
here by somebody.

A cloud of white blossoms
settles over the water,
against the Ohio river shore.

The first weakness is I love to gamble.
The second is I am no good at it.

The gods created this world
as a game. Even ants play
with flower petals.

Resist what resists in you.
Become yourself.

THE SUMMER WE LONGED FOR COMES

It is ninety five degrees in the cottage kitchen.
July, not a breath of air.
My wife complains,
Sweat is coming out
of me everywhere.
Her shoes are full of sweat.
I can hear it in her step.
I have always listened for news
of whatever is passing by:
a comet's dust, a tattered season,
a grease monkey's jabber,
the signal of her callused heel.
I smell the musk of a drunken priestess.
She plays upon the windchime
my noisy bones make.

I say this as plain as I can.
Sweat is the tears of cold stars.
Sweat fuels the pearled engine of the mollusk.
Sweat is the magic marker on the ghostly chalkboard.
Sweat is a newborn child in the halogen family.
Sweat is the ink of saints.
Sweat is a holy bead
at the back of my wife's knee.

FIRST BLUES FOR MY GRANDSON
—for Liam Michael Ragain

You found your first breath in Laguna Beach,
salty, troubled air.
The Pacific is cold along that coast,
even in summer.
You calmed when your father first touched you.
An hour later, as you lay beside your mother,
he gave you your first music,
mini bandbox recorder by your wet combed ear.
Miles Davis, *Kind of Blue*,
hot, jagged, fluid bite,
stuttered horn brew.

Miles was born in the same town
as your father Sean, Alton, Illinois.
Miles walked Belle street down by the flour mills,
listened to its dope racket,
the Piasa bird clutching at his shoulders,
the muddy Mississippi river carrying away
the bad silver from every account.

Miles played the way
he wanted to be, whispered
to you the first hour of your life,
his sullied breath through the devil's horn,
teaching you to breathe in beat
with your own heart,
to talk with your own shadow.

Little Miles. Long Miles.
Ten miles of hard blue road.
Breathe deep, Liam Michael.
Listen hard.

JIM HARLEY BUYS A NEW HAT

He was christened in Thessaloniki
as Dimitri Andrus Halembackus.
His father wanted him to thrive in America,
to melt down in the iron pot.
His new world name is James Harley.

Now, at fifty three his heart is a busted two barrel carburetor.
His knee caps are blue; his toes are toadstools.
No circulation. No prevailing westerlies.
He walks with a hickory cane.
He has lost forty pounds somewhere.
He has died four times this year
but won't leave the grounds.
When I met him five years ago in Greece,
he could bend a parking meter to the ground,
dip a cigar in gasoline
and smoke it down to the nub,
while goat dancing on the hood
of a police car.

This afternoon the Ohio glacier retreats
for an hour or two.
I dig him out of his house next door,
for a drive across Portage county,
R & R for winter's frostbit soldiers.
We park and walk a long fifty feet
from the car to the Ravenna Goodwill.
Digging in the bargain bin,
Jim finds a hat for fifty cents,
olive drab, military bill,
with the words EMS Bootcamp
black stenciled across the front.
He holds it up with a grin.

EMS Emergency Medical Service Bootcamp
EMS Ecstatic Merger Simplified Bootcamp
EMS Easy Money Spent Bootcamp
EMS Emma's Marvelous Shoes Bootcamp
EMS Elementary Music Shines Bootcamp.
EMS Elastic Muscle Shenanigans Bootcamp.

EMS Eternity's Moonstruck Simpleton Bootcamp.
Pick one.

I gotta big head, says Jim.
I got thrown out of a New York
haberdasher's. They couldn't fit a head like mine.
Today it fits.
We pay up and step out, unarmed,
into the pale, slanted December light.

I want to walk a little while
with this goodwill man.
I want to rattle Christmas with him,
in my house.
I want to eat some portion of his death.

WHAT IS THE MATTER OF SPECIAL WONDER
—for Riley Danielle Ragain

A new grand daughter
is born this Sunday, June 13,
just after noon, Portland, Oregon,
by cesarean, cross cut.
Riley Danielle Ragain.
Danielle after my father's first name Daniel,
my middle name and my great grandfather Ryan's
first name, all men who awoke
in the lion's den, on a stone floor.
Riley, its roots in *rile,*
to stir, to bring forth what is inward.
The world you want unfolds from where
you stand, from what you do.
Live the life of Riley
with a full heart.

My gift to you, your first birthday,
is this Wurlitzer accordion,
the size of a small wheelbarrow,
pale pearl buttoned and black toothed,
bellow winded, a stomach Steinway.
Slovak squeeze box, forger of dirges,
chaser of devils with its reels and jigs.
Say it, *Wurlitizer,* and a carousel begins to turn
in your head, the silverware in the drawers
becomes windchimes, your socks crinkle with music.

This belonged to a woman you'll never meet,
Edna Hershey who lived on Chestnut street
here in Kent, lived into her nineties.
Everyday she played this accordion,
morning songs to welcome the sun over the trees,
sunset sonatas to make the fishes weep.
Its tones are honey rumble under the graveyard,
the big boned whistle of the dervish.

My gift to you, Riley Danielle Ragain,
is an engine lifted toward the almighty,
a pearled sword against what lives below.

Riley, cleave the rock with your song.
Rock in the road. Rock in the head.
Rock in the roll. Rock in the heart.
Prisoner's black rock on an iron chain.

Learn to play loving kindness.
Play equanimity. Play compassion.
Play joy with and for others.
These are the houses of the heart,
where the heart makes its home.
In every house, make a place
for crazy love.
Never turn away crazy love,
all your life.

When you are strong enough to lift it,
put your breastplate on.
You are a soldier in the army of the Lord.

COBALT MOUNTAIN

My grandfather's name was Chester Arthur Totten, named after a president. Nobody does that anymore. He was a farmer, working a little more than a hundred acres in southeastern Illinois with a team of draught horses, Pat and Mike. There is a photo of me, a year old, sitting on the broad back of one of them, supported by an unseen hand. The horses were replaced by a third hand Farmall tractor. Machinery was hard to come by during World War II. My grandfather was austere and humorless, not hard but gruff. He had hands big as toilet seats, broom stick thick fingers. I heard him laugh only once. I was five. We were picking wild blackberries along the fence rows. They were plentiful then before the deluge of herbicides. We both had full buckets of berries, coming down the muddy bank of a little pasture creek we had to cross. I scrambled down first, splashing to the other side. Grandad followed, making it halfway, slipped, stumbled and landed on his butt in the foot deep water, his bucket emptied into the creek, his bib overalls filling with water. His face was brick red. He did not curse, a God fearing Methodist. When he tried to struggle to his feet, his bibs ballooned with water. Down he went again. This time I laughed. He glowered. I shut up, figuring a whipping for my impertinence. But, he began to laugh, then roared... and splashed like a schoolboy, drained his bibs and sloshed home with me and my full bucket. Now, I understand how he was strange to himself and dear to himself, caught in the frame of a body and underneath all of this is nothing.

Two years later, Grandad Chet died of stomach cancer. He'd taken Milk of Magnesia as long as I can remember. Out behind the farmhouse rose a blue cobalt mountain of broken Milk of Magnesia bottles, about three feet high. Everytime he finished one, he smashed it on the pile. It was beautiful, his cairn of agony, his cobalt blue big rock candy mountain. Dad took me out to the farmhouse a few days after Grandad had been buried. It was early December; the house was empty and unheated. Dad went in first; I stuck close behind his legs. We got as far as the kitchen. In the middle of the room sat two big zinc washtubs full of shit and blood and wadded bed sheets. I hid my face against Dad's coat. I knew how hard he had died. Grandma Blanche moved to town. The farmhouse was torn down, then the barn. The Kentucky coffee tree was cut down, along with the walnut and the maples. The well remains, if you can find it, clean, cold, extending all the way to the iron ball at the earth's core. The cobalt blue mountain was leveled to make way for the corn and the wheat.

MAC LOJOWSKY, THREE SHEETS TO THE WIND, CALLS FROM A PHONE BOOTH IN DIRTWOOD, ALASKA, AND LEAVES THIS MESSAGE.

Mac has been working on a fishing boat
off Alaska, weeks on cold, mountainous waters,
parka men dangling lines six hundred feet
for halibut, pale bottom dwellers
the size of a car hood, nosing the shelves
the light never reaches.

Mac has come ashore in what sounds like
Dirtwood, Alaska, in the small, beer blurred
voice on the answering machine.
Says he's turning straight north, walking
and hitchhiking to the Arctic circle.
He wants me to write him a poem
to shout to the Arctic sea.
I listen to the message a dozen times,
trying to hear the name of the town,
Dirtgood, Durwood, Durcould. Finally,
it has to be Dirtwood. Sounds like
the oldest, most god forsaken place
on earth. Mac is going on to the top
of the world till the borealis
cooks his balls like hard boiled easter eggs.
Till his magnetic poet's tongue freezes forever
to the iron pole marking the true north.

In the dark, before bed, I punch up
the message one more time.

> *Major, this is Mac.*
> *I'm in Dirtwood, Alaska,*
> *chasing the fish.*
> *Haven't caught any.*
> *That's okay.*
> *Heading to Anchorage next,*
> *then up to Fairbanks,*
> *then hopefully across*
> *the Arctic circle.*
> *But, I'll be getting you*
> *a line or two somewhere*

on down the road.
Take it easy.

There must be no way to take it easy
above that last border. You have
to take it harder and harder. Whatever
you know outside the circle you must
leave behind when you cross over.
The blood slows and slushes.
Words break up in your mouth.
You begin to think with your feet.
You eat your own breath.

Mac made it as far as Coldfoot,
the Dalton highway, the Arctic Acres Inn,
the northern most bar in his America.
A last beer, two days standing by the road,
permafrost thumb pointed toward Santa's workshop.
Not a single truck. Mac turned back south,
the circle unbroken.

This small poem arrived too late. It is not enough,
against that immensity.

> *Old Mother,*
> *I am coming down*
> *to find you*
> *on the black ice floor*
> *of the world,*
> *to lay my head*
> *on your cold breast.*

THE STARS OVER ST. JOHN'S CHURCH HOLD THE
AUTUMN CINCINNATI SKIES TOGETHER/A WEDDING POEM
—for Jim, Pam, Luchia and Nina/October 12, 1996

The four brightest moons of Jupiter,
Io, Europa, Callisto and Ganymede,
are named after lovers of the god Jupiter
(as are all of its more than sixteen moons).
Io is covered with volcanoes,
Europa with ice.
Callisto is pocked with craters.
Ganymede, the largest moon, is water and ice
bound to an iron core.
A love is a moon, not a sun,
bound, extending the common life,
holding light, looking
both away and toward that which binds it.

Around the equator of Jupiter
swims the Great Red Spot.
Larger than the earth itself,
it is a storm in Jupiter's clouds,
a gaseous quaking, a shifting shape.
It swells and recedes.

The four bright moons orbit in a plane
of Jupiter's equator, so they appear
strung out in a line
drawn through the planet.
Some have seen them with the naked eye.

There is nothing we may call our own.
A union is but a dream.
The meeting and the parting
is as when clouds having come together
drift apart.
The task, the marriage, is rendered for its own sake.
It is the task which is served.
To serve in this way is to be free.

Serve. Be free. See the moons for yourself. Avoid the authorities.

TRUSTING THINGS AS THEY ARE

About 12:30 every afternoon, he taps his way to the front door of the Tost Cafe in Thessaloniki. He comes from the Greek School for the Blind across the street. He is not a ratter tatter who uses his stick to assemble the world in quick little sketches. The cane doesn't find his way as much as it clears it, as if he is fencing with an opponent who always gives ground. He does tap the front door glass once or twice to announce his coming. Once inside, he folds his sectioned cane with a snap of his wrist and pockets it. Then, this big tulip bulb of a man begins to sway back and forth on his heels and booms, honks, hollers, with courtesy, *Kalimara, Stella.* The waitress Stella answers with a cup of coffee and takes him by the elbow to an empty table. *Efcharisto, Stella. Te Kanis, Stella.* He loves to say her name, *Stella*, holding the last syllable with his tongue, making the la trill before releasing it as if it were a tiny yellow bird. A tiny yellow bird going home to a star, crossing years of darkness and cold to return. When the tulip man sits, he sings quietly to himself, or to Stella, in a quiet, childlike voice. He makes a shuttle with his left hand, each finger in order touching the thumb, and back again. Perhaps his hand is singing. Or counting heartbeats, his, Stella's, mine.

MORNING DREAM SONG
—for Terre

In the dream, I was at a table,
with three other men in business suits,
pointing pencils at one another,
an English department committee meeting.
I was hungry. A hand to my right
passed a tin of small yellow mints.
I refused and passed them on.
I wanted to tell them about my swim
that morning, all around the lake
where I was raised into this world,
Vernor lake back in Illinois,
how I was buoyed by the waters
of kindness, held in its arms.
I rose from the table, turning
like a dervish, my arms extended.
Then, the room tilted. Out the window,
the lake was just below us,
its green depths, blue shallows, sandy shores.
I was about to tell them.
Look, there I am. Not here. There.

The phone rings.
I spin upward and find myself
in bed, tangled in flannel sheets.
It is my friend Terre from Cleveland.
Did I wake you? she asks.
I don't know. Out the window, what had been lake
is a backyard strewn with yellow leaves,
bare trees, gray slate roof.
Can I come visit Wednesday, she asks.
I can't find my voice.
It is following me back from the dream.
*Do you want me to sing to you,
a Quaker song I sing to my daughters
Hannah and Lucy when they are waking?*
Yes, I say.

> *Arise and shine
> for the light has come*

and the beauty of the lord
is shining upon you.
Arise and shine
for the light has come
and the beauty of the lord
is shining upon you.

All morning I swam,
spreading the waters with my arms,
around the blue lake.

Even now, I am wet and shining.

BUSY WITH SURRENDER / WINTER SUNDAY

I catch one winner today, simulcast
on my living room TV, from Turf Paradise,
a horse named *Citizen Crane*.
Splayed marriage of words, Orson Welles
tethered to a flock of Chinese cranes,
dragged across a bare landscape.
CC. C.C. Rider. Don't you do me,
momma, like that easy rider done.
Heart Crane. Citizen Hart Crane
from Garrettsville, Ohio, just up the
Cuyahoga river. Stephen Crane ate
his own heart, in the desert, his hometown.

I didn't leave the house till late afternoon,
making my snowy rounds out Summit street
to Ravenna, around frozen lake Hodgson,
back to Kent. I find my friend John
sitting at his table, eating basmati rice
and broccoli. Health, mid winter
yim yams, the iced up white lymphatic rivers.
We talk about it on the wander back
to Ravenna, past the Walmart Taj Mahal.
Asthma is a ghost who sleeps in the attic
of the rib cage. Diet, the word
comes from the Greek *diata* meaning
a pattern for life. Diet is more
than what goes in your mouth and comes
out your butt. We both grow weary
of the palaver about the same time.

We used to haunt the race tracks together,
perfumed with parimutuel whiskey, holding
our empty gamblers' bowls up to heaven.
Beautiful courtesans danced barefoot
on the car hood, every long mile home.

The body is that part of the soul
we can see. The car is another body
I wear, metal shirt and pants, tires
sure tread shoes, the windshield big

eyeglasses. This old Nova walks me
around Portage county's concrete trails.

I pull up to John's place. The tulip tree
next to the driveway has started its
January sap push into fuzzy gray buds,
slowly walking into bloom.
John slams the car door, waves, steps away.
I am alone again in my bodies,
out into the streets.

LUNGS, CAVE, MOUNTAIN

If you want to achieve a certain thing,
you have to become a certain person,
but then you won't care about
doing that certain thing

      —Dogen

This late spring day is murky with green,
thunderstorms building off to the west,
nimbocumulus walking through southern Illinois,
raking the empty house of my childhood
with tines of hard rain, rolling over
the muddy Wabash river into Indiana, across the cut bank
White river, onto the till plain of Ohio.
The certain person I have become today
makes raisin toast, holding down the pop up release
of our broken wedding toaster.
I boil green tea, its bitter morning slake.

Wilma Harley calls from the Alleghenies
to confess a dream. She is from a long line
of Scottish witches, bred for dark prophecy.
She dreamed herself driving
her little red Geo Metro,
me in the back seat, head back
gasping for air.
At that moment, I was in
Cuyahoga Falls general hospital
in the pneumonia tank, intravenous truss,
hot wired to steroids and bacteria whackers, room 239.
And with Wilma, in her witch wagon,
in a tunnel through a mountain's stone heart,
no headlights, no air.

It is getting darker here on East Grant street.
I bear down on the lines from Dogen
to renounce the striving for certain things,
for certain persons, the striving to be.
I must drop these as a man
drops a heavy stone he has been struggling
to carry across a field.

This is not my stone, not my field.
These are not my shoes.
This is not my hat.
These are not my lungs. I am not them.

There is another air to breathe, polar, crackling with light,
born in the cave of the Nagasaki bear,
in the blueblack heart of the thundercloud.
I was born on that mountain.
There is my home.

A WEDDING STORY FOR BEN AND KATHERINE
—Read at Christ Episcopal Church/Kent, Ohio/July 13, 2002

Late morning, midsummer lunch under
the striped canopy of our back porch,
a table spread with fruit, chicken,
cashews and bing cherries, cut melon,
slabs of warm, fresh bread, the ruby heart
of wine beating welcome. To our friends,
Daniel and Margaret Bourne, led down the driveway
by their newly adopted son, Afzal, his lock kneed,
get out the way, just short of two years,
world walker strut. In February, Daniel and Margaret
flew to Moscow, then across the snow fields
of the Urals to Tobolsk, a village in Siberia,
an orphanage where they claimed him from among
the hundreds. They had only a few ragged moments
of videotape, a smile, a child's glance
at a camera's cold eye. It was enough.
They brought him home to Wooster.
Afzal had never been loved,
the hard law of the orphanage.
He had no things of his own,
the communal property of the orphans.
No room of his own, only his name
and a handful of words
in his native Russian.

Today, Afzal is held safe in his new family,
Margaret and Daniel, with us, Lu and Meg, in the
green carnival of northeastern Ohio summer, roses,
clematis, dragons who snap, the broadswords
of sunlight cutting across the porch.
Afzal stands beside me, wedging a handful
of watermelon into his mouth.
Less than two, he is already a little man,
heavy boned, square shouldered, from a people,
the Tartars, who swept across the steppes into the valleys
of sleeping tents, men who hacked open
the coffers and set aflame the watchtowers.
He is sturdy enough now to ride bareback,
trampling wheat, splashing across snowmelt streams.

Another handful of watermelon and he squats
beside me on the porch, knees to chest,
a slight grimace, a lop sided grin, a grunt.
He stands and wanders off, loaded diaper,
a trickle of skyline chili down the back
of his leg. Margaret picks up the full
saddlebagged little warrior by the armpits,
swings him down to the sidewalk, strips shorts,
shirt, diaper and paper towels off the little
chili dog. She wrestles the green snake
garden hose and turns it on Afzal,
belch of cold well water. He never flinches,
this Siberian snow boy. Stamps his bare
feet and laughs, little moon flower
gulping the rain, breaking open the clear
spring at the heart of every moment we live.
Afzal squeals, dances, tumbles.
Margaret hooks the hose to the sprinkler
out in the yard. He gallops through the
upside down rain, the silver lattice, butt
bare, his laughter and straight ahead pecker
pointing the way back and forth through the water,
in the sunshine falling from whatever heaven
there is, in the grace of things as they are.
Afzal commandeers the sprinkler, turns it
on us, peewee gotcha now super soaker.
Surf's up in the backyard, cold kiss
of well water drawn from the secret
midnight rivers far below us,
the bone fire hell always six feet
beneath every step. We each take
our dousing, bow to the little Tartar king,
his silver sword.

None of us knows the source of the splendor
that spills over us everyday.
Ben and Katherine, take your dousing.

Refuse the towel. Stay wet.
When you don't know what else
to do, bow your head.

It is your gift to others.

The clarity of the heavens, the milky river
of stars, all look down on the backyard mud
where Afzal dances.
Where you are is more than you want.

Everywhere is darkness, save small lanterns
hung here and there in immense, cold chambers.
Make a bonfire together.
Be warmed by the burning of old and new found
stupidities.

To pledge your troth means to put
your truth in peril. Attend to the unfolding.
You have come a long way to stand here together.

Find a failing in the other you cannot
bring yourself to love. Befriend that.
It is a secret door that opens onto
a garden.

It is all God's work, the watermelon's sunset
split open, the miracle of bread, the play
of rainbow light through the spray. There is
a present glory in raising the fingers to the lips.

Never forget Afzal, now John Carter Afzal Bourne,
another of the best men, one day in a Siberian
orphanage, at a long table waiting for the bread
to make its way down the long line of hands,
faces and empty plates. The next day he is
in the arms of a father and a mother, carried
home over snowy mountains, across an ocean.
That is the way it is. Trust what has chosen you.

Untangle the old knots. Someone else tied those
for you. Tie this new one here, together, today.

Ben and Katherine, enter this marriage as if
you are crossing great mountains
and going home.

The Inward Field

Zeus sought to plumb the center of his new world.
It is the fate of the gods to know.
He brought forth two eagles and set them free,
one from the east, the other from the west.
The point at which their beaks met
he marked the axis mundi, the belly button of creation.
Delphos, where I once stood to listen
for the gods' smoky answers to my own riddle.

Sheila, Cisne wisdom mother, understands
what we want is beyond all striving.
She told me, *The eagles' beaks*
meet in each of us, somewhere.
Rumi says, as he leans on the shovel,
Out beyond ideas of wrongdoing and rightdoing,
there is a field. I'll meet you there.

It is that inward field
across which the eagles fly.
Where the beaks touch,
there I will meet you.
All the sweet, high yearning
in us is for that place,
beyond the mossed stone,
the bright skin of objects.

Perhaps we are standing in the place we yearn for,
we already have what we desire,
and the eagles have touched and gone.

AGNES BRAUN'S CHURCH IN THE WILDWOOD

My old man liked to drink his Sunday beer in Teutopolis, Illinois, a small Catholic farming town dominated by a church steeple surrounded by a corona of honkytonks. His bar of choice was Braun's, catty cornered from the church, first stop for the penitent after mass, plain wood floor, bare yellowed light bulb noosed from the ceiling, a six foot bar womaned by Agnes Braun herself. She always wore a house dress, flowered, slip slappy house shoes, in her sixties for what seemed decades, smiling, idle, suffering, ready for the devil or the parish priest to come through the door thirsty. A two by three-foot portrait of heavy lidded J.F.K. hung behind the bar. I always think of him and Agnes as a couple. There were several tables and chairs, newspapers strewn about, a candy bar rack and no nonsense. You didn't need a sign to know that. The old man drank Stag beer in a gold can, with a black, glowering, antlered creature on the label, a cheap beer with a hoppy, dry bite. He drank beers the way most men drink shots, banging them down and waiting for the flash, then the thunder. He wanted the waters of forgetfulness in a six pack. Stag beer at Agnes' was as close he could get. The old man loved that honky tonky, the refuge, the certainty that everyone there was slowly burning up together.

I got to going up there when I turned eighteen because the bars in T' town would serve anyone, figuring we were all God's thirsty children wandering in the desert. I made spring runs up through the farm country forty miles or so to T' town, the fields all swelled up and stinking with green. Braun's was tough for me to get into. The front door had a big step, but I'd grab the door frame with my left hand and swing my stiff right leg up and over, like a determined drunk getting on a horse. Agnes liked how I did that, greeting me with a big, slow grin. She knew me as Dan Ragain's boy. The old man had moved to Florida in 1970 and started a new life in a neighborhood of small pastel houses with tinted windows. I kept finding my way to Teutopolis. First, I'd pray in the church, alone in the back pew, renouncing the devil and all his works, tattooed by the light streaming through the stained glass windows. Then, I'd walk over to Agnes' beer chapel.

The history of Teutopolis began when two German Franciscan monks rode horses with gold filled saddlebags, from the east in the mid 1800's, searching for ground for a seminary. They found it here in the Illinois flatlands, at the edge of the great prairie. Sometimes, as I sat in the back pew, a brother, a monk, would tend to the altar, his smallest gesture magnified in a great arch of the church. I longed to wear his robe, cinch my waist with his rope, put behind me the carnal wars, the secular racket, and lean, with full trust, on the everlasting arms. But, across the street, beckoned that single light bulb in Agnes' bar. When I hoisted myself through her door, the holy water was still cool on my brow. In my thoughts. In my speech. In my heart.

The old man died in December, 1990, in his Florida kitchen, stood up to make some coffee and just kept falling. That summer after his death, I drove coast to coast, Baltimore to Oregon, to wash away my stupidities and old grief, to give it to the road. On the way west, I swung through T'town. I hadn't been there in years. I spent a half hour in the great cool belly of the church, the acid bath of tears and prayer, then across the street to Agnes'. It wasn't Braun's tavern anymore, but a pizza and draft beer joint, named Snazzy's, quack quack and free popcorn and new Nashville country slick twang. I asked the blonde farm surfer girl about Agnes. *She retired a couple of years ago and sold the business. Probably down at her house right now. Go down to Sunoco and take a left. A brick house with flowers all around.* When I pulled up, she was in her housecoat, working in her garden. *Hello, Agnes, it's Maj.* She hurried back to the house, hid behind the half open front door. She wasn't dressed right, she said, to talk to anyone and besides she had to get ready for church. I shrugged goodbye and walked toward the car when she called out. *We used to have some good times at the tavern.* When I looked back, the door was closed.

Back at Snazzy's, I ordered two shots of Early Times, the old man's favorite Kentucky bourbon, mine straight, his with a side of water. I told the sparkle-plenty wheel-of-fortune barmaid that the shot and the water was for my old man who would be along shortly. I couldn't wait, the road is long, but would she please leave it there for him. I had scattered his ashes in the muddy Embarras river just east of Teutopolis. No marker for his life, just an unstrung rosary of whiskey shot glasses left on the bars across the grid of America. I figure some of them are still there years later, semper fidelis bartenders wiping around them, an empty stool. Little votive glasses. Little grief bells. Bugeyed spectacles for the stone blind. The glassblower's tears.

VALENTINE'S DAY CARD TO JAMES BEAM
—Venice Café, February 14, 2003

I am a little drunk.
Sometimes I wish I were born a little drunk.
A tiny whiskey pump, no one could see,
one I didn't find out about till I was, say, sixty.
A whiskey gland at the base
of the skull, a slow drip of sour mash,
a distillation of god's grain, into the brain, the groin,
spirits caught in a jar.
They wake up the blood,
bang around in the living room of the heart,
turn on that mortal light,
thirty five watts, just bright enough
to call out a shadow.

We sit at a long, smoky table,
puzzling about love, why it comes for us
or leaves us alone.
None of us knows.
I say this: offer yourself early.
You won't know how to do it late.
This is whiskey talk on a saint's bloody day.
I believe my own words.

Broken long stem cross, knotted fingers,
the bright tent of skin.

The gift of the empty basket is the basket.

THE BOW, THE WOW, WITH BROTHERS

When I park my old white Nova in the driveway
and climb out, the two neighbor dogs, a couple
of houses down, start up, overgrown golden retriever pups,
tangled winter coats, flop earred, bored and fenced.
I bark back, a guttural *boyz, boyz, boyz.*
They warm up and volley. I gurgle and growl.
Woof, woof from the pups. I *rowl, rowl.*
They quiet, sitting side by side, staring through the fence.
I finish with a tooth gap sucky whistle.
The pair sends over a half hearted *woof*
as I close the screen door to my big dog house.

I am washing my hands at the sink
with that iridescent, pink pearl jam, antiseptic squirt soap
when a train whistles and rumbles by, along the Cuyahoga
at the end of the block. The dogs begin to yap,
then go wacky as if in pain, *yip, yap, yowl,*
a doggy chorus, back and forth with one another.
As I reach for the clean towel, a big bubble of yelp
rises in my throat. I am ready to howl with them,
a two legged whoop brother, hairy under the arms,
the nose, around the balls, tailless.
The train rolls on south. The dogs trail off.
I turn out the bathroom light and keep the peace.

My crutches are my walking dogs,
twenty years old, a yard sale find,
now duct taped and Elmer glued,
shin splinted, rust bolted, the way I like em.
They walk. I follow my skinny wooden dogs.
Tall dogs. One legged dogs. Four legged man.
I got to find my bark.

From the rinzai zen teaching that thorny question
no one gets past: does a dog have Buddha nature?
I don't know. Does a man have dog nature
and therefore Buddha nature? You bet Buddha
is a bulldog, big jowls, heavy ears, no bark, all bite.
He is sitting dog. He walks by sitting.
My walking dogs are named left and right.
They are all I need.

SEARCH FOR THE WISE MAN

The morning glories are losing their colors,
regressing to white, the pale seed.
It is not from the cold. It is late.
I have been dreaming of driving west,
toward the mountains, toward Oregon
where my son lives, in the Willamette river valley.
He windsurfs the Columbia river.
I drag my left foot now when I walk,
leaving a trail of half moons.
I am easy to track.
My car has three new tires and one bad one.

Yesterday, along the Cuyahoga river in Mantua,
a fisherman told me Lake Erie is now as clear
as well water.
You can stand on a pier
and see twenty feet to bottom.
It's the Zebra mussels from Europe.
They've cleaned up the lake,
One vast filtration system.
Everyone thought that meant disaster.

I find a horse for the day,
in the thirteenth at Thistledown,
allowance company for fillies and mares, 3 year olds and up,
at 6 furlongs, 8-1 on the morning line.
The horse is named *Zen's Endless Angel.*
Rilke tells me every angel is terrifying.
Every angel is a blanched morning glory
shining over clear water.

COLD MUSIC WALKS DOWN FROM THE NORTH

The sun has eaten away the last of the backyard snow.
Time to cut back the brown stalks of the mums.
If it goes undone, they will bloom anyway.
I have been clipping coupons this gray winter.
For one dollar I receive one jumbo package
of Trip-L-Crop climbing tomato seeds,
basketball size tomatoes in ninety days,
less if I start them inside early.
It is best to start early — and stay as late as you can.
An Amtrak tour across Canada,
free information, the craggy Laurentians,
the shining wheat fields of Calgary.
A brochure for a visit to the Pigeon river fish and wildlife area,
Dept. FS, Box 71, Mongo, Indiana,
teeming with smallmouth bass and trout,
canoeing through hardwoods, gravel shoots.
The Cuyahoga river by my house
is still black with winter.

Last week I left Steve Melton,
my tall friend with a fresh shave,
in Riverside cemetery, section 15, lot GG, grave 57,
that first night in the cold ground,
his sunglasses in his left hand.
I should have stayed, built a bonfire
on his grave and kept watch till dawn.

His mother Christine later found a viola
in his closet, hidden in a corner.
He didn't play one, she said.
What the dead play
we don't know,
a cold finger around the lip of a whiskey glass,
a tire iron on the side of a dark house.

They Have the Same Source, But Different Names

At the Northfield, Ohio Goodwill store,
when I bring the three used books
to the register, the sugar dipped,
torpedo pocketed manager, with her moussed
bushy flat top crown, welcomes me
with a hello pilgrim smile and a question.
You got any discounts?
The books figure to total less than two bucks.
I don't know what she means.
I'm sixty, I tell her.
Got a golden buckeye card? No.
Got a driver's license? I do.
And show her my grimaced division of motor
vehicles plastic laminated photo, birthdate, Sept. 15, 1940.
OK. She rings up a 10% discount.
That'll be $1.87.
This is my first discount for having lived this long.

It is raining, the second day of a late spring.
I have been wandering from Goodwill, through
Salvation's Army, searching for what I don't need,
wasting time I don't have. She places the thirteen
cents change in my palm with a receipt.
I stand there. I hear something far inside me,
the shifting of old timbers in an abandoned mine,
a faint voice traveling for years through a maze
of dark tunnels, longing to be heard. I can't think
of anything to say to her, but I won't leave
until she knows me for the wingless, earthbound
creature I am, my mother's skinny heartbroke
child, until she knows me underneath
the breastbone where I live, alone with the alone.
I am staring at the floor, counting
black and white tiles, chewing my tongue
when she says, *Eleven more years and I'll get my discount.*
Then I'm gonna quit and write a book.

What about? I ask. I won't let her go.
My husband. He died last year of lung cancer,
lived a life of sex, drugs, smoke and rock n' roll.

43

It killed him at forty six.
That last day I told him
he either had to get a miracle or die.
I was glad when he died.
I couldn't take it anymore.
I'm gonna write a book.
I'm gonna read it, I tell her.
At least, I'll have an audience of one.
Count on me. I wink.
I am about to tell her
my old man had died of emphysema,
leaving, on his kitchen table, a full carton of Camels
which I donated to the boys at the corner tavern.
I can't find the words.
Too much smoke in the world already.

Instead I ask if any accordions
ever come into the Goodwill. *Rarely.*
I want to write down my phone number
on a scrap of paper and my name.
I want her to know my name.
It's Maj, jam spelled backwards,
I'd grin, leaning on the counter.
Call me as soon as an accordion,
any accordion, shows up in your store.
I am the accordion man.
I couldn't say that.
I don't know how to play an accordion,
even a squeeze box,
though sometimes at home,
I dig out one of my basement accordions
—I keep buying them—
lie on my back in the living room
and spread the bellows,
a long raspy sad groan, a squawk of notes.
That's enough. I just want the gods
to know I'm here.

One day, I'll come back to the Northfield Goodwill.
There it will be, on the glass counter, polka ready,
my pearled lung box piano, my deep water bagpipe.
The rainy day widow will wink.

I've been saving this just for you.

My books and I find our way out the door.
Giles Goat Boy, hardcover, The *I Ching*, the Legge
translation, and *How to Master the Game of Poker*.
More pots and pans for the mind's kitchen.
I forgot to ask his name, her husband,
whether any of these were his books,
the man who chose between death and a miracle.

POEM TO BE READ AT MY SIXTIETH BIRTHDAY PARTY
—with thanks to Kitte Lyons

Thank you for coming today
to honor me, to give sanction
to the skinny drum I am, buckle and leather,
a slow walk across these years,
to bless me with the honeylight of your eyes,
to fill me with your breath.

Thanks to the tuba player
honking on that brass morning glory
wrapped round his chest.
I don't know what you paid him.
It wasn't enough.
Thanks for the gift of the goat,
bearded billy the kid, chowderhead
of roses and laundry lines.
Thanks to those whom I see everyday,
who live along the river with me
and tend the traps.
And to those who are at the edge
of the woods and cannot step forth,
my father in his burlap robe and wooden shoes,
my brother young gone blues man
green hide cured.

Thanks to the dervish children
with their may pole reared toward heaven,
salamander feet, rainbow spin.
Your dance scabbards the blade.
And to Spoony Paine, Wabash river rat,
rotten potato sprouting bearded brother,
here to goose the archbishop
and steal the wiener from the bun.
I am glad you've come back from hades' coalmines.
To my friends the poets,
each head a walnut clasped
in heaven's cracker,
each head singing what is gone, is to come,
the ghost in the bread box,
the burning rose of love,

the arterial map of the underworld.
The ribs shape a cage,
but the heart flies away.

Thank you for the poets' soup today,
iron pot, the two handed spoon,
hacked potato, shucked corn,
grief grease stock, the giants's
beans, crushed nightshade apples,
rosemary's tears, a flick of ash,
buckets of river water.
Let's eat big steaming bowls.
Then light a fire in the backyard,
a beacon on the great plain,
a burning boat, a hosannah.
In it I burn the mistakes,
the affronts, the regrets,
how ever I might have disrespected
your soul, its shining path
across the waters.

Each of you has appeared to me
in some guise, as have I to you.
The time is near when each of us,
in this plenitude, must become beggars,
when even the stone hearted turns
toward the pilgrims' home.
This I will remember,
the shake of each hand,
the brush of your hair,
the quick light between us.

Inside each of us is
a solitude, an unborn child
sleeping in the belly of a cello,
a dragon fly caught, midflight, in anthracite.
It is to that we look when we love.
Forgive me for not offering
that part in myself to you.

I now abandon the midnight excavations,
miles of scaffolding and shafts, dead ends.

I couldn't find it, the tin cup
of burning tears from which I long to drink.
Let us build a bouquet of kites
to fill our skies, strap drunken rockets
to our backs and fly, holding hands, downrange.
Serve the soup, pass the jug.
Let the brass notes of the drunken
tuba morning glory man climb toward heaven.
Let us, each by each, in our own time, follow.

IRON ROOSTER

The Easter phone rings.
It is Margo, small boned
Italian woman about whom
the stars turn in perfect
circles. She is playing
the Chinese wooden flute
in a six piece band.
The erhu player is a cold
mountain man come down
to the lowlands to make
his music, a single cat gut,
strung from toe to wrist.
He plucks his songs
with his teeth.

They have been chased out
of the willows, the clouds.
Where can we play? she asks.

Come play at my house.
Take off your shoes.
Dance on my chest.
Strike up this band.

With her back to me,
hidden in song,
Margo begins to play,
softly, clear as water.

In the darkness,
over her head,
a life searches for a form.

I am feeling my own thick hide,
as if for the first time.

WHEN I DON'T KNOW WHAT ELSE TO DO

The first day of summer
we uproot the sweet annie herbs
in the plant barrels.
They have outgrown themselves into seed.
A tumble of yellow jacketed hornets
fills the air, the top of their mountain
blown into the heavens.
They fly like drunken fish, sperm,
blind lost pilots from the galaxy
that labors inside this one.

Spring is gone. Nothing works.
My lessons fumble along.
I am trying to learn to bow,
to give myself up.
I empty myself out the top of the head
and right myself, ready to be filled.
I must be prepared to bow,
even in my last moment,
to pour the old rancid coffee of self desire
onto the ground where I stand.

READING MY POEMS ON ASH WEDNESDAY, WITH DRUMMER HALIM EL DABH

—Room 310, Student Center, Kent State University

Reduce my spirit to trust.
Then it would be spirit.
The words of my friend Ted Lyons.
I say this to myself everyday,
to steady myself against my own stupidities.
Reduce my spirit to trust.
I want it more than breath.
That little dirt road between trust and spirit,
I walk it back and forth with my wooden bucket.

These poems are fumbled songs,
half baked pies, the cart driver's argument
with the donkey, love's little cello,
no bigger than a shoe, laces strung.
I saw away with my clumsy bow.

What are you listening for,
all lined up in chairs?
You should be dancing,
stepping on one another's feet,
introducing yourselves as you really are.
You should be giving away
what you want to keep.

The northwest Pacific tribes named it *potlatch.*
Their shamans envisioned a dying world.
Spring could not find its way back
through the mountain of things.
Potlatch. You give me a gift,
I give you more. Six salmon
and a telescope calls for, in return,
a kayak, four goats, three hubcaps
and a flashlight. Which gets you
a bolt of silk, a missionary's
black hat and silver crucifix, a singing seal,
a dozen bearskins, nine paddles and
fifty scrimshaw brooches.

It goes on, this giving, till no one
has everything. No economy,
just abundance, the wreckage of ownership.
Possession becomes a bitterness.
Then, one morning, a child,
standing alone on a mudflat,
begins her song, words no one
has heard before. People gather,
barefoot. Spirit and trust join hands.
We start over. Always, we start over.

Halim's drums are skins
stretched over emptiness.
What are we?
Skin stretched taut over cheekbone,
rib, knee, belly. What do you play?
The whack of the living hand on dead skin.
Who plays you? The dead hand on
the drum that you are.

If you are sleeping upright
in your chair, it is not you
we will pester with words
and drumming.
May you be rocked in the cradle
of your dreams.

Someone here in this room
is an apple, a winesap,
a golden delicious.
We pick you.
Halim and I play upon
the skin drum of your ear.

Morning Note to My Friend Virginia Dunn
—*October 22, 1943-June 26, 2004*

Two days left in the old year.
The Cleveland *Plain Dealer* front page
trumpets: the wait is over.
The Browns make the playoffs.
Helmets, pigskins, punts, touchdowns,
touchbacks, offsides, two minute warning.
The war moves to Pittsburgh.

I brew tea,
no more whiskey and coffee,
rust in the belly.
Irish breakfast tea, the red bloom
of Assam in the clear cup.
I drink the tears of my people,
counties Shannon and Cork.

I sit down with a haiku,
Basho's three hundred year old
hard tack biscuit.

> *Now being seen off*
> *now seeing off — the outcome:*
> *autumn in Kiso.*

Over and over, I stumble on these lines,
which grow tangled and humpbacked across the path.

> *Now being seen off*
> *now seeing off — the outcome:*
> *autumn in Kiso.*

Count the day's income as the gift of hours,
gray light, talk, repair of what is
broken, music, black letters
on a page, breath. The outcome is
what is, *tathata*, thusness. Nothing
we add to. Nor diminish.

May the tongue's butterknife,

the hand's hatchet,
the broadsword of the arm,
cut a window in the heavy sky
between us.

I want to see you on
as far as I can.
I want to be seen on by you.
A farewell, a greeting, each day.

It is autumn in Kiso,
winter in Kent.

THE PENTECOST

It was a Pentecostal tent meeting, a prayer service, a summer revival, 1951, Springfield, Illinois. The Reverend Oren Jaeger, dark eyed, natty wide lapels, Bathsheba's dream boat, a hands on healing man, was in evangelical bloom. He looked like a Kennedy, a toothy cerebral animal in a tailored suit, a commander in heaven's army. The Reverend Jaeger paced the stage, Bible in his hand, calling up the spirit, subduing demons. I was down in front with my mom and dad and Aunt Julie who could speak in tongues and smelled like sourmilk perfume. We had come for the healing. Reverend Jaeger opened the show with a cautionary tale against drunkenness and the inevitable folly which accompanies it. He paced the stage and thumped the Bible with his knuckle. He told this story. There lived a good man not far from here, he said, who obeyed God's laws, shouldered his burdens and praised his Lord. But, he strayed from the path and embraced the demon of drink, the serpent of suds. That man suffered a change. He lay down in the barley and the hops — and with the women who paint their faces and follow the camps. He became a recruit in the army of John Barleycorn, an air spirit in love with earth. Down he went. One Sabbath he drank up his store of beer and sought more. Champagne Velvet was his poison. He drank it by the case. He swilled his Champagne Velvet though the children had neither milk nor bread. He bathed not; he cared not. He honored neither his father nor his mother, his wife nor his children. His soul paddled like a lost duckling on a sea of Champagne Velvet beer. That Sunday he wrestled the car keys from his weeping wife and sped away across the county line where the bars were open on God's day. He wove in and out of traffic, passing cars, cursing. Reverend Jaeger paused, raised his Bible. It was head on, he intoned, head on, another pause, a head on collision with the object of his folly, a truck, not just any truck, a beer delivery truck, loaded with, pause, Champagne Velvet. When the police pried him from the wreckage, they found, driven through his chest, like the vampire he had become, a long pole with a banner bearing the words *Champagne Velvet*. So are the wandering brought to judgment, so does the lost sheep find his way home. My mother, then in the spangled bloom of her mid thirties, loved Reverend Jaeger, though she never said as much. Nor should she have.

In the healing line that night of the Pentecost, it became my turn to suffer the laying on of his hands. In front of me, an old woman with her arm in a cast had raised that bum arm, waved it windmill fashion and broke out into tongues, the gibberish of praise. Then, I was wheel chaired up to the Reverend Jaeger. He put his soft, cologned hands on my head and demanded that the devil come out of this boy, that I be released and made whole, that I stand and walk, nay, run down the gangway for the glory of God the father who has not left us. I struggled to stand. I could not. My legs wouldn't work. The Reverend allowed sometimes the healing took time. He was convinced the healing had begun. His lieutenants shuffled me on down the line. Another pilgrim took my place. *Now, who do we have next?* asked the Reverend, God's sweat on his brow. At the time, the fault seemed mine. I had been unable to open myself to God knocking on the door. I had disappointed those who love me. Now, I understand there is no blame in this.

That was the summer of the northern lights, all over the midwest, great bars of electric orange lights that spiked crystalline. It was the summer of the flying saucers zipping through the electromagnetic tumble, scaring cows and air force colonels, spawning stories of men from planet X inseminating housewives with seed pods, then whisking away. That night, driving back from the Springfield tent meetings, in the 27 model A Ford, me asleep in the back at three a.m., Mom and Dad saw the saucer. It came down in a farm field, just off route 130, a carousel of blue and orange lights, utterly silent, tracking the car for some minutes before whirling away. We weren't the ones they wanted. Our lives were small. My father swore my mother to secrecy; the Ragains were poor, but we weren't crackpots. We drove on south to the lake cottage, to the fate of my father, his heart frozen since childhood, to the green death of my brother. We drove away from the pillar of the Pentecostal fire that rose out of Springfield, the Aurora Borealis whose homing signal had called forth the whirling galleons of other worlds, lives we would never know, lives that would track us and fly away, drawn back to the womb of a mother ship.

When I turned eighteen in Terre Haute, Indiana, I drank my first beer, a warm quart of Champagne Velvet. I climbed a long flight of stairs in a whorehouse at Second and Cherry, climbed with a railing, without wheels, guided in the night by a beacon, a single red light bulb. I was sure footed. The next morning, I thought of the Reverend Oren Jaeger. I know he did not understand the nature of God's love for me. I have never learned to speak in tongues. I am whole, though crooked. I am upright, though I sit. I carry no stake in my heart.

LOVE'S DARK NOISE
PORTSMOUTH, OHIO / JULY 26, 1993

Steve Melton calls from Cleveland
to read me his poems singing the life
of one of those old bib overall bastards
in Big Sandy, Tennessee, where Steve was born.
One of Big Sandy's ten honest men,
shit ass whittlers who ride the liar's bench
till the truth walks by.
Steve won't let them die without a hearing.

He's broke, left his last dollars on Mitzi's pool table,
drinking and grieving over a friend of his.
A man Steve calls Chief, down in Portsmouth,
shot himself a couple of days ago,
in his living room where he and Steve
used to drink beer and cheer Sunday Browns football.
Before Chief put the gun to his own head,
he shotgunned his twelve year old daughter Alicia.
Police found her in her bed.
Scioto county children services officials
had been trying to remove her from her father's house
and turn her over to her mother.
Somethin must have snapped, Steve said.

I have been haunted by these stories
all my life: little throats cut,
heads held under the bathwater,
pistol barrels in the mouth.
When the devils kick in the door,
no man can turn them away
with mumbled prayers and crossed sticks.
I don't know what it is that snaps,
the tight rope we walk barefoot from birth to death,
the piano wire strung taut inside the skull,
the sour heart's one gut string tuned wrong.

The Chief's raw soul is tunneling
through the sunset, sky, up over Portsmouth,
howling like a skinned dog.

THE OLD MAN SHOPS MONKEY WARDS

Tonight, I was shopping the liquidation sale
at Montgomery Wards, State road.
Monkey Wards, my grandma Blanche called it,
back on the farm in the late nineteen forties,
the brick thick catalog on her lap,
her dream book by the kerosene lamp.
Now, Monkey Wards has been snuffed
in the corporate wars, at the age
of one hundred and thirty two.
Yes, we have no more bananas today.
I bought a pair of fake Rockports from a grim
saleslady, 40% off the original $29.99.
I was untying the knot after trying
them on, the left one, when a scratchy,
disembodied voice announced over an
intercom speaker ....*Dan Ragain....Dan Ragain.*
Please report to electronics.

My father's name. Dan Ragain.
Gone ten years now from his little green house
on Freedom Way, Seminole, Florida.
The electronics department is one floor down.
Maybe the liquidation sale has called out
the old man's ghost to buy a radio at 40% off.
In his last years, he loved to sit up all night, listening to
sad heart, twelve step talkshows, rightwing
looneytoons, UFO abductees, cancer cures
from outer space, after midnight gossip
with graveyard janitors, third shift nurses,
the sleepless, lonely, coffee-cooked moon crew.
Where would his ghost find money?
He left his wallet on the kitchen table.

I thought of riding the elevator downstairs
to look for him or ask if there was a salesman,
an associate they're called, with that name.
I couldn't do it. I didn't want to know.
I loitered around the jewelry counter
and found a tiny crucifix on a sterling silver
chain, formerly $29.99, now out the door for $4.00.

The chain is tarnished. I can fix that.
The saleslady said, *You got a bargain there.*

Monkey Wards. Primate Specter Wards.
Haunted Iron Rail Hospital Wards.
Ghost Walkers On The Radio Waves.

Sales. Final Closing. Fixtures Included.
Everything Must Go. Liquidation.

ENLARGE THE PART THAT BELIEVES

The three primordial afflictions are embodied
as a bird, a snake and a wild pig:
greed, aggression and sloth.

The bird perches on my left shoulder,
chirping separateness, mine, mine.
The snake I wear as suspenders
to hold my bare butt off the cold gravestone.
The wild pig I ride for a dusty mile.
Then the razorback straddles me.
Where am I going like this?

The golden finches titter and fuss
over the niger thistle.
Each is greed's tiny winged sunboat,
hauling away the mountain
of black thistle, an eyelash at a time.
Each finch is an empty singing bowl.

The rattlesnake of aggression,
the bristled root hog of sloth,
have not found me today.
It is all beautiful, winged greed,
the burning, golden tears
of some nameless, dying neighborhood god.

A MEETING THAT IS SECRET

In my first grade class, Central school, Olney, Illinois, the girls played on the east side of the school grounds, the boys on the west, divided by metal fencing. The girls left for their recess early and returned before we did. They were already at their desks when we filed by to find our seats. All of their faces watched the door through which we tramped, that field of sunflowers greeting Helios. Their attention made my stomach muscles tighten and tremble. I don't remember when I first did it, but in the excitement of the girls' eyes touching us, I took to spitting on my hands and wiping that masculine shine on my brow and cheeks just before I entered the classroom. I even adopted a peewee, hands-in-the-pocket swagger to accentuate the glow of spit sweat, to show the girls that I was even then my own man, not a hostage to Mrs. Nichols and her reading, writing and arithmetic. I would not be taught to the tune of a hickory stick. I wanted the girls, especially freckled Wilma, to acknowledge me as an immortal animal, a terrorist of the heart who would not submit to reason nor seek consolation. Now, as I say it, it may seem to you no more than a preening, shitheaded plea for attention. Maybe I have never gotten past this moment of yearning.

Later, I watched my father spit on his Marine Corps dress shoes and Kiwi polish them with a chamois, the skin of an animal. Wilma and I finally swapped spit in her kitchen after she'd grown up and got her own apartment half a block from Central school. She spent afternoons sunning herself in a backyard chaise lounge, shorts and tube top. She had, by then, freckles the size of cornflakes. She made her own suntan lotion of olive oil and iodine. The sun found a way to get through.

MEMORY IS THE MOTHER OF NINE MUSES AND ONE DEAD COWBOY

Another gray winter afternoon, Saint John's children's hospital,
Springfield, Illinois, polio rehab ward, 1951.
Snowscape windows, muted rooms, low hum of dolor.
A phone rang, doors, hurried footsteps.
The nuns hustled us out of our beds, onto gurneys and wheelchairs,
down to the recreation room. *Surprise, we have a surprise.*
He's coming, the old German nun winked.
I thought she meant Jesus whose bloodied, thorn crowned image
adorned every wall. I was terrified. I wasn't ready for the Second
Coming. *No*, she scolded. *It's that movie star cowboy, Gene Autry.*

The nuns got us lined up, row after row. A hush.
Then, spurs and bootheels in the hallway.
All of us turned to watch him jingle jangle in,
white Stetson, sequined cactus on his chest,
gold braid, silver buttons, twin pearl handled pistols.
He stalked in as if it were a Hollywood movie set,
ready for Black Bart to spring off one of the gurneys,
forty fours blazing. He walked among us, dispensing
smiles and autographs. I pulled the sheet around me
and held out a tablet and an orange crayon.
He wrote *Gene Autry* in a big, loopy scrawl,
then shook my small hand. His hand was pudgy,
his fingers stubby, his nails manicured.
I didn't know ding from dong, but when we shook
hands, I knew for certain he'd never punched cattle
or slapped leather.

I never really liked his Saturday matinee shoot-em-ups,
with his doughboy smile and oinky voice.
When I strapped on my own cap pistol, I became
Lash LaRue, his bull whip crack, or the masked man
Durango Kid, with his double life, or ,usually, Billy the Kid,
that plug-em between-the-eyes left-handed gun.
I never ever pretended I was Gene Autry,
the singing cowboy who couldn't carry a tune.
Even then I knew who I didn't want to be.

When he got too old to ride, shoot and fake-romance
the western belles, he turned to California real estate,

stockpiled a fortune and bought the Anaheim Angels,
a genial potentate of the board till called
to that other home on the range.
During the 2002 World Series, his heavy jowled face
was pasted on the digital board beyond centerfield,
bigger than any screen he'd ever ridden across
on his faithful steed Champion.
His widow was on camera every minute in the late
innings, final game, dressed in a red blazer,
surrounded by other corporate weenies in red blazers,
falling all over themselves to pat the widowed CEO
on the back. Jubilation in heaven. The Angels won the series.
Gene Autry may be the archangel Gabriel's kid brother,
but he was never a real cowboy.

I carried the autograph around for maybe twenty years,
a scrap of tablet paper, his orange crayon name
folded and tucked in my wallet, proof for the nay-sayers.
I don't know where I lost it, a vacuum cleaner,
a landfill, a black hole. I'd like to think I dropped it
on a heartbreak street where a pretty woman picked
it up, wiped her tears on it, daintily blew her nose,
wadded it and tossed it away where it was snatched
on the fly by a lovelorn sparrow who carried it
in his beak, like a crushed blossom on winter's
bleakest day, to his beloved who took him
to her breast and held him there as long as we
can hold anything or anybody. This is silly,
I know, but we must dream grandly in our lives
that we not be diminished when we awake.

Somewhere, not far from here, this day, held safe
in the boughs of an evergreen, is that pale, orange
streaked flower, little morning glory of welcome,
little evening glory of forgiveness, bloom blown
from the lips of Aphrodite, Gene Autry's
autographed snot blossom of love.

If you can believe this,
you are the one for me.
I believe in you.
I don't want your autograph.

That was more than fifty years ago.
The nuns, the good sisters of Saint Francis,
led us in applause as he stood at the door,
waving goodbye, *adios little wranglers.*
He took off his big white Stetson,
held it high for a moment.
Then, he was gone.
We heard the bootheels, the shing
of silver spurs down the hallway,
faint and fainter,
then a door open and close.

A Hungry Ghost Surrenders His Tackle Box

My friend Bill Hupp leaves this week,
a year's stay, Zen Mountain monastery,
nestled in the Catskills.
He must surrender his things before
he can give himself away, cut his ties
to the world, gray house on Longcoy street,
green Ford, Taurus bachelor's kit and kaboodle.
He must now trust the sangha,
the community with whom he will train
to live the four noble truths,
to dig through the compost heap
of his suffering and cart it away.

This rainy March afternoon
Bill lays down his burdens at my house.
I am to find solace in attachment
to what he must renounce.
A two foot stack of *Tricycle*,
the Buddhist review, thousands of bent
word keys to the Pure Land, how to shoe
the windhorse, how to jumpstart
the dharma in your neighborhood.

He hands me a sheaf of his own
pissed off, gotta bless you anyway poems,
fuel for his heart's fire.
He drags in a rolled up, inflatable
rubber raft, a ten footer, heavy duty,
Lake Erie tested, with red oars
and a handy foot pump: three hundred steps
should do it. And Bill gives me his tackle box.
I have never heard of a man
surrending his tackle box,
short of the death bed.

Fishing is an attachment which he must sever.
Otherwise, he'll remain a hungry ghost
hiding a can of worms, sneaking out of sesshin
to fish the monastery pond.
I accept his gift because I must,

a big, multiple drawer Plano stuffed
with plastic worms, crusty jars of pork rinds,
jointed minnows, silver bucktail spoons.
I open it once, then consign it to the basement.

Belongings, the little one word book of law.
We must be our longings.
I don't know another path.

Bill, don't forget to come back
for what you belong to,
rubber raft, tackle box, words,
the rest of this stuff
which, as the Buddhists teach,
are phenomena that rise and set
only in the mind.

Late Summer Rust Work

My last day at the Illinois summer cottage,
I begin body work on my rust bucket 86 Chevy Nova,
duct finish tape and black primer paint, layer after layer,
along the wheel wells and rocker panels.
The tool is a blue Brillo pad,
a box of fifteen from the dollar store.
The rust never sleeps.
It chews while I rest.
By nine a.m. the day steeps in heat,
no breeze, baked Illinois August.
The cicadas turn over their dusty engines
a couple of revolutions,
then trail off into silence.

Behind me, the crunch of gravel underfoot.
a sandaled, smiling neighbor woman
has brought me a jeweled gift, a jar
of blueberry-lime goodbye jam.

On honey wheat toast,
it will be my sweet tart raft, my sunrise kayak.
I clamber aboard and drift a little further
down the muddy river on which I was born.
She presents me a pint of pickled
long winter green beans, kissed by garlic,
piqued with dill, the broth as salty as dried tears.
Each bean cracks like a cinnamon stick.

One icy midnight, I will tip back
the jar, drain the moonshine brine
and taste the faint drunken laughter
from her garden, weedfilled, spent.

The Carnival Geek Parts the Curtain

The Richland county fair was always held the second week in July, the baked heart of southeastern Illinois farm country summer. It was an offering of the fruits of harvest to Demeter, goddess of the seasons, breads, pies, zinnias, peaches, zucchini, festooned with award ribbons, blue, red and yellow. Livestock shows with 4-H children leading the lambs, calves, pigs, to the fatal show ring. On the midway: lemon shakes, nickel pitch, elephant ears, gaggles of bare midriff teenage sirens, platoons of horny Marlboro boys. Spin the color wheel, hit your number, pay off in packs of cigarettes (gambling for money was illegal). The rides lit up the countryside for miles, the ferris wheel visible above the dark trees. The octopus, with its neon arms pitching and dipping, at the end of each tentacle a pod of terrified faces. The baleful two headed hammer, a rocket from hell that circled and twisted in the same motion. Everywhere we stepped ran the ground wires, the black, wrist thick electrical cords that carried the carnival fire lighting up the sleepy little municipal park. *Watch where you step*, dad said, *those wires are hot.*

The midway. Sometimes mom and dad would slip me a little money and, though I was only seven, let me wander away on my own. I always made a beeline for the sideshows, where the dogboy roamed and a crazy man swallowed fire. I paid a quarter to witness a blonde woman in a sequined two piece climb inside an orange box about the size of a steamer trunk, slotted with holes. A tall man with slicked back hair and pencil mustache —he was supposed to be a pirate— thrust sword after sword into the slots, hard, bang against the hilt. Why would she do that, climb in there smiling, when she knew the pirate guy was going to run her through ten times? And why didn't she cry out? For another quarter, the horrified assembly could come up to the stage and peer down into the open top of the death box. Everyone paid, looked down, grinned, shrugged, shuffled out of the tent. I was left alone with the killer and the dead lady. *You wanna see?* he asked. I couldn't make my mouth work. He took my quarter and picked me up round the waist, gently, holding me so I could look down into the death trap. There she was, hunched, knees and arms against her chest, sword blades at every angle. She could turn her head ever so slightly. Caught in a thicket of swords, she smiled at me in reassurance, the moon faced boy peering down at her. He put me down and began to pull out the swords, carefully. Then she was free. He took her hand, steadying her as she climbed out. When they smiled at one another, I realized they must be husband and wife. I remember wishing I were their child, a small pirate assistant in this death defying show. Maybe he could draw me a mustache. Maybe I could hand him the terrible swords one by one.

On down the midway that summer, I met the geek. A crowd had gathered in front of a tent on which was emblazoned, in wondrous detail, *Wild Man from Borneo*, with a hairy, barely erect creature loping off into a gaudy green jungle, terrified monkeys clinging to tree limbs. The barker, a skinny fellow in lamb chop sideburns, was conjuring stories of his capture. How it took ten men to get him in the cage, how he wanted his supper alive. From inside the tent, as the barker paused, came knee knocking growls. I paid my two bits and pushed in with the rest of the herd. In a roped off area crouched the wild man from Borneo, a black man of fifty or so, greasy thick hair, khaki work shirt and pants, rheumy eyes. He bounded toward us. We fell back. Then the barker stepped into the danger zone, poked at him, provoking another snarl. The barker asked for another quarter to witness something still more awful. We all anteed up. I pushed to the front. The wild man reached into a crate and by its feet pulled out a live, squawking chicken and brandished it over his head. He danced with it, mumbled incantations, sang softly to it, stroked it into quiet. Into quiet. He bit off its head, waved the thrashing chicken in the air and spit the head into the crowd. Blood splattered the chiffon dress of the girl next to me. She screamed into tears and pushed her way out of the tent. He waved the chicken around, threatening us with it till the chicken stopped jerking. He stepped to the back of the tent, tossed the chicken aside, turned his back and took a long swig from a Vitalis hair oil bottle. It was the same stuff my dad combed into his hair. Vitalis with the secret ingredient V-7 (and alcohol, that spirit). I was no more than six feet away. I could read the label. He finished the bottle, tossed it after the chicken, and stepped into the jungle, the green closing in around him.

Next to the geek show was another tent, another sideshow, through the side, where the wound enters, not main street, but the alley, the side street show, the tent of the arcane. Herein was the world of the beautiful bearded lady pictured on the poster: bosoms, bare belly, whiskers. Mom and dad caught up with me as I stood wondering at the barker. *Come see the half man, half woman. You won't believe your eyes.* Dad told me to stay right there. He and mom were going in to have a look at this lovely freak of nature. Could I go? Of course not. Their eyes were furtive when they emerged from the tent. *What was it?* I asked. *Oh, a person with a man's thing and a woman's thing dancing around*, dad muttered. That didn't help much. We trudged back to the car, me wondering if the bearded lady was maybe the geek's wife and whether they knew the pirate and his blond sword dodger wife.

The carnivals still come to Olney. The Richland county fair still cranks up the second week of every July. The sideshows were gone by the mid 1960's. The ministerial association rose up four square and denounced the sideshows — including the bare titty dancing shows — as a profanation, an exploitation of the unfortunate, a demeaning of the very community which licensed such activities. Goodbye to the Queen of Sheba, to the alligator boy, the armless singing mother of five, the yogi who ate broken Coca Cola bottles, to the two headed fetus suspended, half smiling, in a glass tank of alcohol. Goodbye to the drunken man from Borneo and his maybe bride, whiskered and double whangered. To the pirate and his sequined love and all their pocket knife kids. Now, it is all salt water taffy, merry-go-rounds, break a balloon, any balloon and win a prize, pick a duck, sign up for a chance at a free water softener. The workers are no longer Mack the knife and tattooed Tina, hot eyed road gypsies, scuffy ex-convicts, but college kids bored with their minimum wage summer jobs.

The last carnival geek I heard of was over in Alton, Illinois. Al Bartle told me he'd seen him bite the head off, not a chicken, but a live snake. I wish I could have been there. All we have left are the old stories, these rituals which speak to an awful unknown in us, abysmal, in the flesh before it became thought. We disguise and perpetuate it everyday. The slaughter house hammer between the eyes of the 4-H blue ribbon steer; the happy meal in a box, surprise toy included. The slit throat of the squealing porkchop. The disembodied voice in the Colonel Sanders drive up box asks, *would you like a 20 ounce bottle of Vitalis with that bucket of dead chicken?* Perhaps it is a profane form of worship, the sideshow church, the killing of the body, the scattering, the marking with blood so the dead will recognize one another. We follow Isis' search along the Nile delta for the dismembered body of her brother Osiris. Will his spirit be whole if she pieces together his body? If I could find that chicken head the geek spit into the crowd, what voodoo, what prophetic cluck? Perhaps it is passion and death feeding on one another. The word carnival signifies farewell to the flesh.

Tierasias, the soothsayer whom Oedipus sought out, was a geek. The story is he, as a youth, stumbled upon two great snake gods copulating in the woods, the polar serpents of this and that, an act forbidden to the eyes of man. His punishment was two fold: he was blinded and he was changed into a woman. He grew old, wandering about Greece in the guise of the other, finding his way with a staff. Witnessing his suffering, the gods relented, in part, and restored his manhood to him. Here is the source of his wisdom, his prophecy: he alone understood the truth of both men and women, and he had witnessed the joining of opposites, the gift of the serpents. In old age, he is depicted as bearded but still with the dugs of an old woman. The gods had marked him thus. The hermaph-rodite is literally the union of Hermes and Aphrodite, two gods twining into one body. The caduceus, that symbol of medicine, is a serpent coiled around a rod which was itself once a serpent. The gods danced in a sideshow tent in Olney, Illinois, till Saint Patrick came, along with the Richland county ministerial association, and chased them out for good.

The hair of Medusa was a mass of hissing, writhing serpents. Those who looked into her eyes turned to stone. Perseus slew her by guile, with the mirror of his shield, and from the severed neck sprang the winged Pegasus. Ascelepius, the healing god, caught the blood of Medusa in an urn. Poured from the left side, that blood slays, but, from the right, with that blood, he brings the dead back to life. That blood splattering the skirt of the young woman next to me was from the left side. I was marked that day and have not come clean. The geek held the stump-necked chicken over his drunken head, a sputtering torch to light the way down the dark stairs to the underworld.

LEARN TO DISDAIN SMALL CONTESTS

My friend Jim Harley was born
in Macedonia, northern Greece.
The Germans fire bombed Thessaloniki.
It was 1944. Jim was two.
He remembers his mother running
with him held between her thighs,
the dark world beneath her skirts,
the jar of her steps, the city burning.
Every generation imagines itself to be the last.
Fifty years later, he lives in a little
yellow house, St. Petersburg, Florida.
His meat heart is half kiwi, half stone.
What is left, you save that
by holding him in the fire.

Orpheus spent his last years wandering in Greece,
playing to the rocks, trees and rivers
who listened gladly.
The mad women, the maenads,
already drunk on blood,
caught him near the river Hebrus.
They tore him arm by leg.
His severed, singing head
they cast into the snowmelt water.
The river disappeared into the earth,
ashamed of the spilled blood,
cleansing itself, surfacing
in the foothills of Olympus, at a sanctuary of Isis.
The scattering, the gathering.
The limbs were collected by the muses
and buried near the Hebrus.
The head of Orpheus
the currents carried to the Isle of Lesbos.
His tongue, the golden bell of the skull, would not stop singing.

If the surgeon priests of St. Petersburg
saw off Jim Harley's blue blood dead feet,
give them to me.
I will dangle them like bad eyed dice
from the rear view mirror.

Wear them round my neck
to keep away the frivolous
and the chicken shit hearts.

Hang them high in a bare tree.
Bury them in the sky.
He is in room 363, bed 2.
His soul is an old friend of his.
His body is adversary.

In his dream, we wander together
out to the killing ground,
where the great beast was gutted.
We walk together in the bone room,
the ceiling of ribs.
This is all that is left.
Jim points up to the terrible poison of the sky.
He is laughing.
His wife has made a little supper
to scare off death,
broth, kelp, lemon, whiskey.
His daughter has woven him a crown
of grapevines and asters.
Aster, the word means star.
Aster is the name of the Minotaur
who lives at the end of the ball of string.

BUILDING THE HALLOWEEN BOAT

My daughter Meg and I set to work on
her sixth grade Halloween project:
constructing a sarcophagus and a mummy.
The mummy is simple enough,
a discarded Barbie doll swaddled in
cotton strips, up to her blue eyes.
The sarcophagus asks more of us.
Let Meg figure it out.
I have too many ideas
about longboats that carry the dead,
Sun Ra bound for morning,
the Viking pyre on the water,
the square nosed jon boat back in Illinois.
Meg decides the sarcophagus must be gold.
Big Lots has only white paint,
eighty eight cents a can, the color of simple oblivion.
Gold is the color of the Ptolemies.
We find it next door,
at Stambaugh's hardware,
dollar sixty nine for a big aerosol can,
enough gold to do a king from head to toe.
She rattles the can and asks
What's that?
A little steel ball, I tell her
and leave it at that.
The sarcophagus is a shoe box,
Gitanos, cheap low cuts.
We crush one end,
bring it to cathedral point
and wrap it with shipping tape.
Later, Meg and her mother will line
the little golden sun boat
with blue satin, mummify Barbie
and pack her off to Davey middle school.

I tell her the story of Ra, the Sun God,
how he lies in his boat, passing
through the dark stations of the underworld,
without pulse or breath,
yielding to the night,

74

about to die and take the world with him.
It is at that moment
the jeweled scarab beetle,
his little scuttling brother
who rides his collar, bites his neck.
Ra awakens, claims himself and the world
from death, stands and throws
the lightning bolt of morning.
Meg sprays an unpainted spot on the shoebox.
How long will it be before it dries? she asks.

After the first flood receded,
boats littered the treetops.
There was nothing to do except wait.
When the waters rose again,
every one of them floated free.

TALKING ON THE BLACK LINE TO ITHACA

Katie Daley calls from Ithaca, dancing with the phone. She has just seen the moons of Jupiter through a neighbor's telescope, blinking like Christmas lights. And on the other horizon, big as a barn, earth's own moon, lone, waxing September stone, the cold backdoor lunar light breaking up on the crater's edge, like snow blown from a roof. Katie says this might be the night of her life, with her brand new telescope eyes. Since her daddy died last year, Katie is becoming far sighted just like him. When she reads a poem, she has to hold it at arm's length or thumbtack it to the wall half a room away. It is all happening so fast, she says. I tell her my hearing is on the fade. I can't hear all the consonants anymore, blank words in the middle of a sentence. Somebody speaks the word *shuffle*. I hear something about a *buffalo*. They say *baloney*. I believe they are confessing they're *lonely*. Last night, at the Dynasty Express fast Chinese food drive-through in Kent, after I had ordered a combination lo mein special, the lady's voice in the static, can-I-help-you box asked me, in a burst of garble, did I want a *leghold*. I am not a wrestler. I didn't order chicken. *What?* The second time is sounded more like *leafmold*. My wife punched me in the shoulder and said *eggroll*. *She is asking you whether you want an eggroll.* Katie says I shouldn't buy food at those damned windows. I need to go inside and talk moonlight and baseball with the cook, swap stories with the baggy pants man who sweeps up. Katie wants to see the rings of Saturn next. *What are they made of?* I tell her debris held by gravity in an elliptical plane, nothing solid you can walk home on.

She reads me a poem about a woman who climbs a honey tree and wrecks a hive, engorges the accordion sized comb as if it were a candied crotch. Katie, almost all of the wild bees in north America were killed this past winter, hives decimated by tracheal mites. Mayan ruins of hives, whole villages deserted. It will take fifty years to replenish the population. How will we remember the taste of wild honey, its combed prism inside the skull?

My father took me with him one cold late fall night to cut a bee tree. He had found it while squirrel hunting in the Fox creek bottoms, had heard the tower of hum a hundred yards away. You have to cut the tree at night when the bees are asleep and after they have been smoked. Dad and his friend built a fire around the base of the dead tree, brush and rags, billows of gray, acrid smoke. They laid into the tree with axes. When it fell, it broke open like a crate. The honey cache was big as a rowboat, the new white comb built on the old blackened wax, tier after tier, encrusted with bees. They hacked away the old comb and filled three or four zinc washtubs with new honey and white comb. It took two men to carry one tub along the frozen, rutted, moonlit road to the truck. We didn't get home to Lexington street till daybreak. My father carried me to bed in his arms. My mother was angry. *Where you been with that boy all night?* I missed school that day, first grade. We spent the next week picking the dead bees out of the honey. I chewed a kingdom of comb, searched for wings and stubbled legs between my teeth. I grew honey headed, jumped over fences, banged into glass panes, walked on my hands, slept in the weeds, buzzed around the neighborhood. We gave away pint jars of honey that Christmas, tied with red ribbon. Mom lined up dozens of jars on the window sills, amber medicine from the gods.

All my life I have been building a hive inside my chest, a golden city of comb. I want to make honey of my old failures. First batch I get done, I'll set it all out in shot glasses, call up family, enemies, friends, Pete, the old walking man down the block, sweet Mardi Gras Grace across the street. We'll all sit down in the dark, close our eyes, do shots of honey and tell one another what we see, how many moons we count around one another's heads.

Katie works tomorrow, cleaning houses. She posts signs around Ithaca. *Have your house cleaned by a poet.* Folks call her to say that is what they have always wanted, though they didn't know it. She won't work by the hour or by the poem. She walks through the house, names a price, no haggling. She won't take money from buttholes or people who hang around to watch her, except for a cello player who practices upstairs. He stays. She scrubs and sings and leaves poems where they'll never find them. People are happy to pay her.

Goodbye, Katie, mooneyed, honeyed and brilloed, princess of the feather duster and steel wool. See you a few days after Christmas. Come to Kent. We'll go down to the open field between Standing Rock and the old cemetery, soak a big gasoline circle in the new snow. Stand in the middle with me. We will light it. And sing.

WHEN HIS BODY TOUCHES EARTH, WE LEAVE THE ROOM

They are getting to know me
here at Cuyahoga Falls general hospital.
The X-rays of my lungs are racked in a file,
the crooked ghost downspout of my spine,
the right lung shifted toward the middle of my chest.
The left is wedged between my ribs and heart,
an old first baseman's mitt squeezed shut.
It is strep pneumonia this time,
bacterial gumbo camped out in the lower lobe,
hunkered around a fire ring of fever.

In the emergency room, at three a.m.,
the nurses string me up to intravenous fluids,
a clear vein of salmeterol, a steroid,
and levaquin, a sweep-the-alley antibiotic.
I breathe an albuterol mist,
drink oxygen through a nose clip.
I am admitted. I admit.
At dawn, I am gurneyed up to room 239.
They draw blood. The sunlight catches
the maples at the far end of the parking lot.

Debbie, rings on every chubby finger,
calls me professor and twinkles through
Easter egg green eye shadow.
As I am fighting for breath,
she bowties my hospital issue gown
and confesses her ex husband always
called her fatty, made her feel awful.
Then he left her and married
a real fatty, three hundred pounds
of shake and bake.
What is it he wanted, professor?
Explain that to me.
I tell her passion is a horse without a jockey.
Debbie winks a heavy green lid and says,
I'll have to think about that one.

Later that morning, Tony, the respiratory
therapist, pops in the room.

78

Are you ready for me to beat on you?
Roll over on your belly.
Tony two hands me like a conga player,
palms slightly cupped, from the bottom
of the ribcage up, two sugar canes
on a hollow log.
Both sides. Roll over on your back.
The closed glove hand left lung slowly opens
to check the hail storm music on my chest.
More breath. Tony is light and sure
on his feet, a black welterweight
pounding the speed bag in a gym.
He is sending messages down the dim
hospital hallway that the white man
is paddling up the Cuyahoga river,
with his cargo of disease, gunpowder,
and the god of the wooden cross.

The second day, the nurses wheel in a roommate,
a soft spoken man, seventy one years old,
John Burkhardt. We nod to one another.
Sharon, the afternoon nurse, slides shut
the room divider curtain.
John has been charged with a stomach ache
and a bloody stool. The penalty is a probe
up his butt, another down his throat,
flashlights in the grotto.
He answers no to every question
the nurses ask. It simplifies his day.
The doctors find two ulcers, treatable.
John gets his walking papers,
his clothes out of lockup.
He shuffles toward the gate.
I wish him good luck and joke
that the food will be better at home.
Not really, he mumbles from down the hall.
May the day never come when my last words
to another human being are *not really*.

An hour later, after the aide has stripped
his bed, a tall blonde nurse, jeweled
glasses and side ringlets, slides into the room

with her blood drawing tacklebox.
She greets me with *Hello, Mr. Burkhardt.*
The bedside manner of an aging porn star,
pancake makeup, tangerine mouth, too many skins.
I tell her Mr. Burkhardt went home, discharged.
Time for blood work, Mr. Burkhardt.
I'm not Mr. Burkhardt.
Which arm, Mr. Burkhardt?
She grabs my left arm, taps a vein,
swabs it with alcohol, reaches for a needle.
She glances at my blue plastic hospital
ID bracelet — Major Dan Ragain.
Crusty bonbon gathers up her blood sucker gear
and quick steps it out of room 239,
without a word or a wink,
a wisp of last year's musk
trailing her down the hall.

My last day in the hospital
belongs to Jesus. I am found
out by one of the halo nurses
for stress management,
a Christian retired RN who
plants herself in the visitor's chair,
a gray cornstalk woman who folds
her hands in her dry lap.
Forgive me, haloed sister, for I
have sinned all my years.
I have eaten the wafers.
Still I hunger. The thimbles of juice
have not slaked my thirst.
We hold hands and pray
inside the circles of our arms.
She speaks directly to Jesus
that he protect me, hold me steady
in his soft eyes, share with me
his sandalwood breath.

The next morning
I am discharged to the backseat
of my wife's Honda, the hospital doors
hissing shut behind me.

I hide under blankets,
a refugee without papers,
Rasputin's last bastard child,
a scarecrow hiding a ripe muskmelon
head, a skinny felon caught cold handed.
Steel horseshoes clatter on the asphalt lot.
Creak of leather, prancing hooves
circle the car.
I make myself small, up in my chest,
rocked in my own arms.

When I awake, LuAnn and I are home
in the driveway, Grant street, in Kent,
a grant of more days, a handful of seasons,
beads on a rosary, passing through
fingers.

Finding My Brother

In downtown Salem, Oregon,
at the Breez' diner,
I buy my wife lunch,
cashew chicken salad, ringed with halved strawberries,
cantaloupe slices and watermelon moons.
She eats in silence, and, as we are leaving,
points to a Mexican grille across the street.
That's what I wanted, she tells me.

In Thessaloniki, Greece,
the Albanian refugee came to my table
and held out his hands.
A young man, hollow eyed, drawn like a bow,
the world's meathooks in his spare shoulders.
I fumbled for money.
The manager collared him.
Later, I couldn't find him on the street
or among the other Albanians bivouaced in the park.
These six years since he came to my table,
he has followed me from supper to supper,
every barbeque, pig roast, bake off.

My wife is sleeping now,
walking barefoot through
corridors of cashew chicken salad dreamscapes,
drumming on melons,
spitting strawberries at the horned moon.
My quarrel is not with her.
What I want her to do
I cannot do myself:
be grateful for hunger, for thirst,
not for what fills and slakes.

LuAnn, when you wake, slip
into that bare shouldered dress,
rust red with painted hibiscus.
Let us empty this day,
wear out the night.
I'll buy you enchiladas,
burritos, tamales, tacos,

chimichangas, sopapillas,
Dos Equis, bottle after bottle.

There is, at the heart of everything,
a nothing for which we starve.

The Dancer Melts in a Candleflame

Bill Kallansrude made a living,
cutting leather soles, piece work,
at the Brown shoe factory on Whittle avenue,
Olney, Illinois, by the B & O train tracks,
shipping American to a barefoot world.
He began there just after world war II,
bought a house across the tracks
and raised a family of seven
on forty five dollars a week.
When the company decided to hedge out
the older employees, his supervisor began to send
Bill's work back to him, how he couldn't get it right.
His last day, Bill rode down the elevator
with gentle Homer Gaddy, his friend
who carried the Nazarene in his heart
and couldn't get it right either.

Bill Kallansrude.
I married his daughter Carole in 1963.
I was as dumb as salt
and believed the kingdom of heaven was within,
marriage a covenant, a rainbow from brow to brow.
Bill's wife Ruth stayed home with a headache
and forebodings of iron gray grief.
He came to the small wedding
in the old Lutheran church in Olney,
sitting in the back pew, hat in his hands.
His hat he wore everyday,
a broad brimmed, soft, Bing Crosby
Bells of St. Mary's fedora.
It protected him and engendered kindness,
a homely crown for his bald head.

Bill kept two dollars out of his weekly paycheck
for saturday nights at the old Eagles lodge on Kitchell street.
He said to me once, with a wink, *son, you see a bottle*
of Falstaff on a bar, remember old Bill. That's my tombstone.
The Falstaff brewery has been closed for decades.
His family shunned him all week because of the saturday nights
when he'd walk home all buckled up with Falstaff,

bang on the unlocked door, break a couple of dishes
and snore his way to morning in his small iron bed,
just off the kitchen.

Before he walked downtown to the Eagles,
he shined his shoes with tears, Zippo smoke and Kiwi polish.
You understand how these three things sing together
and the spear can never pierce you.
Bill Kallansrude was a dancer.
In his baggy khakis, rayon shirt and whistlestop hat,
he floated across the dance floor on his wingtips
like a man in love with air.
And he lifted those whom he held in his arms.
They lined up, doctors' wives, meter maids,
monkeys' cousins, to be carried across
Illinois hardwood skies.

Bill Kallansrude drew his last breath
in a small bare room, the new Olney hotel,
two blocks north of the boarded up shoe factory.
I went there to clean out his room
with his son David, to haul it away,
his two cardboard boxes of history.
You go there now, the First National bank
has built a drive up branch office
on the corner where the hotel stood.
When you punch up your secret ATM code,
your express money in multiples of twenty
delivered by steel fingers,
remember Bill Kallansrude died there,
just up above your head.
Say his name. Hum a tune. Shuffle your feet
before you put your money
in your pocket and drive away.

I don't want to stir in you grief you can't use
but to awaken one of the jewels
you carry in your chest.
I stand here for Bill Kallansrude,
the dancer who talked with his moonshined shoes,
in this aerie from which he flew.

The Fruit Will Ripen By Itself
—*For Virginia Dunn On Her Sixtieth Birthday*

Sixty Buddhas in your backyard,
lapis lazuli, humming medicine light.

Sixty brass begging bowls, full of emptiness.

Sixty snowballs in a hot iron skillet.

Sixty bearded irises, skinny, rainbow haired
old men, gathered to sing at your back step.

Sixty crows, in a tall bare oak, laughing at
the pilgrim who wears his jockey shorts as a
skullcap.

Sixty shoes, lined in a row down your sidewalk.
No two match however hard you try.
The lean pig did this, now free from his hungers.
This is an act of friendship.

Sixty smooth black stones to throw at the first
quarter moon, low in the sunset sky, the new moon
with the old moon in its arms.
It is not as far as it seems.

Sixty lightning rods, birthday candles on the
roof of your house, catching fire, one by one,
from the northern lights.

Sixty sycamores, parchment barked, along the
White river, southern Indiana, as they lean
toward the water, their hair trailing in the
spring floodtide, drinking what it knows.

Sixty thoroughbreds, in a live, not a dead,
heat for first, each nose touching the
finish line at the same moment, dropping
every tin hearted gambler to his knees
and crowning him with the belief he has sought.

Sixty little poems inscribed on rosetta stone
ground wafers, communion with the first word,
with the last.

Sixty shots of Jameson's Irish Whiskey at
Ciccone's tavern, the waters of life,
marriage of the earth's tears and the grains'
broken heart. Let us drink them together,
our shoe-laces tied in one hard knot
under the table. Let our closeness be such,
you drink, I get drunker. Put it on my tab.

Sixty little wooden boats, shingles, tree bark,
lighted with votive candles, pushed out into
the Thanksgiving current of the Cuyahoga river,
carrying away the cargo of last year's grief.

Sixty kites to fill the sky over your house,
stemless flowers, hollyhocks, dahlias, daffodils,
snapdragons, riding the updraft, catching the last light.

Sixty butterflies, jeweled moons in orbit
around your head, around the beautiful flower
you are, a tulip out of which to drink this
day's holy wine.

Sixty begonias, a phalanx of bloom, four petal
faces whispering, not begonia, but stay.

EZZARD CHARLES DEFENDS HIS TITLE IN TAPIOCA FEVER TIME

A big fever walked through me,
in the late summer of 1947,
carried me to a polio quarantine ward
lock up in Centralia, Illinois,
a dormitory of iron bunks
and children burning.
The weeks broke up into little islands
of tears, thirst, blur and hunger.
My parents were permitted to stand
outside my window a few minutes each day,
hands against the glass.
I couldn't eat, pushing away the trays.
All I wanted was the cold tapioca pudding
my mother kept in the fridge
in a big ceramic bowl,
the antidote to every poison.
No tapioca in the fever jail kitchen.
Then, one 104 degree night,
an orderly shook me awake,
propped me up with a pillow and fed me
cold tapioca with a slow spoon.
It hurt to swallow.
I closed my eyes and tried to find my way home.

Down the hospital hallway,
from the lounge, a radio.
I could make out the reedy voice
of Don Dunphy, a boxing match
from Madison Square Garden.
It had to be a Friday, the Gillette blue blade
Friday night fights that Dad and I listened
to every week on the Motorola radio.
The piping jockey-thin voice of Dunphy,
through the fever hum, announced it was
fifteen rounds for the heavyweight championship
of the whole world, Joe Louis, the Brown Bomber,
against Ezzard Charles, the Cincinnati Cobra.
Joe Louis was the people's champion,
the thunderhanded son of a cottonpicker.
Joe can take you out with either hand,

Dad had said, feinting with his left,
crossing with the right.
That night, Louis was a plodding shadow
in the hospital hallway.

He was to die broke, thirty years later,
owing the IRS over a million world war II dollars.
His last job was as a house greeter
at a Las Vegas casino, sitting in a wheelchair,
wearing a white Stetson, making the players welcome
with a soft shake of his big, hard hands.

I struggled to swallow and listen
to the far away lilliputian voice calling
the opening bell, the early rounds,
the curious radio shorthand making visible the unseen.

> Louis backs Charles into a corner
> and lands a left to the head,
> a right to the body
> and takes a hard right to the head.
> Louis ties up Charles.
> Charles digs a left to the body
> and staggers Louis a short right.
> Louis backs away, circles to the left
> and finds Charles with a jab.

The voice got smaller.
I sank back into the cave
with its pulsing hot lights
and cold footing.

Ezzard Charles had finessed his way
to a unanimous decision
and was booed by the crowd.
Charles was knocked out the following year,
dethroned by Jersey Joe Walcott,
one crushing left hook,
the night the lights went out in Philadelphia.
You go to Cincinnati, look for
Ezzard Charles avenue, downtown off I-75,
white letters on a green sign,
an arrow pointing the way.

AGONIES ARE ONE OF MY CHANGES OF GARMENTS
—Whitman

A pair of goldfinches chitters at the feeder, interrupting my prayer.
Psalm 143:8. *Teach me the way I should go, for to you I lift up my soul.*
The male is a bold, clean edged yellow, the female smaller, light brown
smudged with gold.

Procne, the Athenian queen, sought revenge against her adulterous
husband. She killed their son Itys and roasted his limbs over a fire,
served them to King Tereus, watching with hard eyes as he ate his fill.
Then, she named his supper. Tereus held Procne and her sister Philomela
at knifepoint till the gods intervened, changing Procne into a nightingale,
Philomela into a swallow, Tereus into a hawk.

The nightingale's song is of the murdered child.
The swallow hides in the tall pillars of the evening sky.
The hawk still hunts in sharp eyed grief.

These finches of gold.
Midas and his hungry queen.
An old pawnbroker and his stingy wife.

MOUNTAIN MAN

Saturday at a garage sale in Brimfield,
I spent a nickel on a three inch plastic
statue of the hunchback of Notre Dame,
the Disney Quasimodo by way of Burger King.
His upturned face gives me his cracked heart,
as he puts his arm around his brother gargoyle
and sighs, *Would that I were made of stone.*
I am that brother.

I set him on the dash
of my worn blue Nova, beside the silver,
laughing, lop eared hoti Buddha,
big bellied hitch hiker.
The bell ringer Quasimodo piggies his hump,
carries it on his back.
The Buddha has swallowed his hunch,
his cold mountain.

I must carry my mountain
where everyone can see it.

Bless me, bury me, sixty winters of snow
on my hump and a gaggle of blind children
sledding down icy slopes of baby's breath.

LET ME NOT BE CURED OF LOVE

This spring, when I made my annual
pilgrimage back from Ohio, I stopped
in Greenup, Illinois, and bought a huge
hanging basket of pink geraniums
for my mother who was waiting on
the front porch for me, as she does
every year. Just before I turned off
route 130 onto our road, I hoisted
the flower basket onto the car top.
It looked as if I had driven five hundred
miles, a one-handed delivery, a cargo
of blossoms across three states,
green tang of geraniums in my wake,
a lotus eater terrorizing eighteen-wheelers
every mile of interstate 70.

Gift, giver, she to whom it is given,
one breath.

The basket now swings from the porch beam,
the planted head of a flower crowned saint.

Always, the work is to remember God.

FOR MY DAUGHTER MEG, GRADUATING FROM KENT ROOSEVELT HIGH SCHOOL

Monarch butterflies find their way,
through days and nights and storms, across the gulf
to winter, sleeping in the dark trees of Mexico.
No map. They know where home is.

Look for your teachers.
They have come a long way to meet you.
An old woman who talks to the wind.
A child who weeps and draws pictures in the dirt.
A beautiful young man, his face painted
in colors you've never seen.
The teacher may not be a person,
but a storm that carries away your house,
a blossoming dogwood that walks about
while you sleep.

Love and death are wondrous gifts.
Few open them.
Don't fail to open the gifts.

Your actions are your only
true belongings.
Nothing else is yours.

Be a love dog. Howl for what you love.
Refuse the chain, the fence,
the little house that keeps you
from the rain.

You are a quick river in a green time,
finding your way to a great sea
that will call to you all your life.
Never forget you begin somewhere
in the mountains, far to the north
where snow and sky join.

IN THE DREAM THERE IS ONE DANCER

First morning in St. Petersburg, Florida,
I am awakened by mourning doves,
in the trees across tenth avenue,
talking softly among themselves.
I climb out of another dancing dream.

A young, black haired gypsy woman
dances alone, a slow whirl,
a dervish of silks, clink of spangled bracelets,
in a dimly lit, stale American Legion Hall.
She refuses every suitor.
A band plays on, lamely.
The drummer can't keep time.
She hears another music, drunken with it.

The dance is a supplication
to come kiss her ribs, each by each,
this harlequin helicopter spiraling
down into the arms of darkness.
I sit flat footed at a long table,
in my hands a small silver teapot.
I have drunk a cup from it; another remains.

I ask the nameless woman next to me
to offer it to the dancer.
She will not accept your gift.
I know I am the other for whom she dances.
The teapot is surety I have come, across the years.
The two cups are the broken ocean rejoined.
I hand it to the doubting, sour woman at the table.
She stands, walks onto the threshing floor.

The gypsy is whirling in her silks,
closing like a lily, fading.

The mourning doves, their liquid tongues,
their deep, rattling coo.

ACROSS TENTH AVENUE / ST. PETERSBURG, FLORIDA

Every evening, I watch, from the second floor balcony,
as the slight, humped old woman shuffles
out of her gingerbread house across the street
to sweep her sidewalk
with a little broom and dust pan,
to rid it of every bit of the day's leavings.
She stands as upright as she can,
coaxing every leaf and gum wrapper
into the pan with little measured pushes of her broom.
Nothing escapes her fierce attention.

I'll sit out here all night and just before dawn,
cross the empty street and lie down
on her concrete, praying my skinny butt
will fit into her little dust pan.

She knows I don't belong there or here.

Old angel, tickle me with your broom.

OUR FIRST BODY IS MADE OF FOOD

Late supper is shishkabob,
chunks of curried chicken,
red bell pepper, sweet vidalia onion,
over a bed of basmati rice.

Around the picnic table,
the children giggle and tease
with boogeyman grimaces, kicks
at the python hiding under their chairs,
stories of abductions by hairy devils,
trapdoors in the schoolyard.
Megan, my daughter, turns round in her chair
to ask me if I am afraid of dying.
No, I am not afraid.
I mean it
here on the back porch, in their company,
under a melon striped awning,
a half moon lighting my bent hands.

Little Sarah tells me
back when the dinosaurs walked the world,
there were vampires.
When the dinosaurs died out,
the vampires survived by getting smaller,
becoming mosquitoes.
The little immortal bloodsuckers
that flap around us.

The voices of the children.
The soft flurry of wings.

SATURDAY MORNING, PROVINCETOWN, JUNE 13, 2003

I still have many things to say to you, but you cannot bear them now.
—John:15

After a week of cold wet wind,
sun breaks out over Provincetown.
Sand drinks the rain.
Grass lifts up its hands.
In an hour, I won't remember
the iron sky, the blood's dull pulse.
The present claims us as its child.

This day I must find a way
to make myself worthy,
not in hope of the gift,
the beggar's bowl extended,
nor in the cultivation of goodness,
on bare knees at the soul's rock garden.
Not worthy of being loved,
rather worthy without merit,
without object, without understanding.
Worthy of nothing.
Worthy as the windfall grape
which knows nothing of its loss
in the sacrament of wine,
then blood.

ZOOT SIMS/QUIETLY THERE

Two a.m. notes of tenor saxophone,
Zoot Sims, Johnny Mandel's tune *Emily*.

Silky chestdrum breath rolls.
Lovely clean brass methane burn.
Cool bone scaffolding.
Marrow step back to earth.

Color bubble opens
like an orange poppy,
held where we can hear it,
fades, last warm light
against bare, still trees.

Quietly there. Quietly here.

Ache of things unseen.

A Poem of Thanks to Jim McCarthy

There is more to the world
than everything in the world.

This cold Thanksgiving day,
as we do every year,
we drive through Standing Rock cemetery,
down to the Cuyahoga river,
to that great rock midstream,
freight car size, its Pontiac face
pointed due north, an ancient council rock
where warring tribes once talked
their peace, weapons stacked on the banks.

A handful of friends, my son Sean, pilgrims all.
We pass a pint of whiskey against the chill.
Standing Rock, my son the geologist pronounces,
is igneous and striated, its base
above the waterline formed of sandstone
planed at angles, the result of
glacial upheaval eons ago.
I contend it fell out of the heavens,
called down by prayers from a dozen
star crazed monks, wheeling in
from Polaris, splashdown in the Cuyahoga.
The same loving argument every year.

We hang the bottle, emptied of spirits,
in the branches of a tree no taller
than a man, leaning toward the river.
In it, we leave a five dollar bill,
for in God we trust, a black stone,
worn smooth by worried thumbs,
a rolled up pack of morning glory seeds,
heavenly blues, a red guitar pick
and, from the little book of the boneyard,
these lines from your poem.

LATE SEPTEMBER, THE SORTING

My friend Pete Leon has booked a flight
to California, to bake his Cleveland bones
in a sweatlodge, to cure himself in the elders' smoke,
to chant open the chest's iron door that love might enter,
spilling its basket of hot fruit, rosebud drunkenness.
Would you like to go? asks Pete.

There is more here than I can do:
paint wood, scrape rust, move words around on the page,
rake, mulch, tend the trellis on which the ghostly lung
flowers vine, the hammer blows of whispered prayer,
the mapping of the unseen, that kingdom.

This evening, driving up Lincoln street, toward home,
I watched the fall sun drop below the treeline.
The light was gone, except far off to the north,
where it fired the ramparts of a thunderhead.
It was, for a moment, a towering mountain range
packed with spectral, pink blushed snowfields
over Lake Erie, the Ohio Himalayas,
himalaya, from the Tibetan, *holder of snows.*

I stay here another winter to hold the snows,
clutching the cold to my chest,
embracing what is.

Know that the heart makes its home
where it must, in snow, in cloud,
in air too thin to breathe.

THIS WATER IS NOT FROM THE WELL

When I plod the L shaped sidewalk
into Satterfield hall, to teach my classes,
I say my prayers.
First to the Christian lord
that my debts be forgiven
as I forgive my debtors.
I want to begin the day broke.
Then I seek the Three Refuges:
in all the Buddhas, held safe in their bellies;
in the Dharma, its shining path;
in the Sangha, the community of unsullied spirit.
I am never alone.
The Three Determinations are the hardest to say.
I cleave to them.
I do not understand them.
Let the mind rest on the Dharma.
The Dharma rest on poverty.
Poverty rest on death.
With the last determination,
I make the sign of the cross
and punch the automatic door opener,
embossed with the stick man in the blue chair.
The door swings out to greet me.
Bless me. Teach me. Protect me.
My last prayer, by the elevator door,
in the narrow hall.

A String of Ordinary Words

When the Samurai walked into battle,
they carried small purses
containing money for their funerals.

The two virtues are *Katannu*,
knowing our debt of gratitude,
and *Kataredi*, trying to repay it.
These sustain the world.

In the beginning, take the teacher as teacher.
In the middle, take the scriptures as teacher.
In the end, take your own mind as teacher.

Soon, like a hair pulled out of butter,
leaving everything behind,
you'll go on again alone.

The Hunchback Comes Out and Rolls in the Snow

I have let my hair grow long here in Greece
and christened myself with new names.
It hasn't helped.
I still walk on my heels and leave
big tracks for the dogs to follow.

In the mountains, the farmers are burning
the fall fields. They drive their little
rusty trucks to the borders, shake
gasoline out of a jerry can
and throw a match.
They are killing the old growth.
Simple as that.

An hour before dark, I wander into
a tiny village named Eliniko, lost.
The road has ended. The only citizen
on the streets is an old German stickman
out to salute the sunset.
He leans in the car window to give
me every wrong direction. *Machts nichts.*
His breath is battery acid.
His uniform is buried somewhere in these mountains.
Members of the Greek resistance
were taken from their homes, out
into these streets, and shot,
in front of their families.

King Philip II of Macedonia is bedded down
in the Thessaloniki museum, just up the street.
His tomb lay unplundered for twenty three
hundred years, till 1977, when a Greek farmer
struck the roof with a spring plow.
They found nobody home,
except in a small solid gold box,
a larynx, decorated with the sixteen pointed
exploding star, sign of the Macedonian kings.
Inside were burnt bones and teeth,
on top of which someone had placed
a wreath of oak leaves and acorns,

in gold hammered so thin
it trembles at the slightest breath.

When his first daughter was born in 315 B.C.,
Philip proclaimed, *May she be called Thessaloniki*,
in Greek, victory over the Thessalonians.
It has always been war ground here.
By 1944, the Nazis had sent fifty thousand
Sephardic Jews and a small nation of gypsies,
in cattle cars, to the death camps,
while I was a boy safe in Illinois.
My own first daughter is named Megan
from the Gaelic for strength and courage.
The same iron rails still run due north from Thessaloniki.

Megan calls me tonight from America,
through the tangle of codes and numbers.
Her voice finds me, through the lines
worked fine as gold hair.
I close my eyes and let her small voice
move inside me.
She is learning to play the viola,
a big wooden tulip she has warmed
with her hands and taken into her arms.

Praise God, mutter the shivering souls
as they duck their heads to go down
into the dark passageway.

Little Victory, pick up the delicate bow,
bear down and play.

Winter Letter to My Friend Jay Holcomb in Yellow Springs, Ohio

I am writing to you from Ciccone's bar, Cherry street, Kent, Ohio. You'd be at home here. The high cheeked barmaid plays George Jones by the jukebox hour. In the john, over the urinal, someone has penciled in *The Wishing Well*. In the wire trap rest two pennies. They have been here for a while. One head. One tail. They wish us well, as they guard hell and heaven. The true guardian of hell is that big, sour, hillbilly girl sitting at the bar with a belt of ravenous dogs encircling her fragrant zone, eating at her life, she ahowl in pain, in song. Guarding heaven is a tiny child, no larger than a hummingbird. Her name is mountain wrecker. Fear her. She is our only death.

This is a gambler's bar down in the old Italian neighborhood, west Kent. Eighty years ago, immigrants lived in box cars, whole families sleeping on the rails. The railroad repair yard is long gone but the tracks still lead to Ciccone's, a mortal ground where you can open a beer and hear the thunder bite. There are no bishops asleep in their crypts under these floors. Ciccone's Ohio lottery number machine is wired into Columbus. This week the super lotto jackpot is just short of twenty four million dollars. All day people have come through the door. The drawing is at 7:30 tonight. I have acted out of the abundance of my heart, as men must, and played the numbers 6, 9, 11, 14, 20, and 32. I hope I don't hit it, but if I do, I'm going to buy a big chunk of the Cleveland Indians, play third base myself and guard the line.

My old man used to say that everything we do wells up out of loneliness, out of the enormous disconnected spaces inside each of us and that's all any of us has in common. I remember the story of St. Francis, how, in his celibacy and his devotion, one winter morning outside the monastery, he made a family of snow figures and declared, *I shall father a child yet.* How I'd relish to see them both, my old man Dan and St. Francis, walk through Ciccone's door right now. We'd drink lonely yellow beer and play the numbers. I'd wet both men down with cold tears and pray them to teach me that trick that I cannot learn for myself: how to work hothanded with snow.

That which is born of spirit is spirit, that which is born of snow is cold.

Forth Sprang Love, the Longed-For, Shining, with Wings of Gold

Georgie Condos rolled into the Acropolis restaurant
this afternoon in his beat up wheelchair.
The word *Action* is emblazoned on the side panel,
underscored with a yellow thunderbolt.
Georgie's people, I've known him twenty five years, are Greek,
from the northern part, Macedonia.
At first glance, I saw the word *Action*
as *Actaeon*, the great hunter of Greek mythology
who drank the spoiled crazy wine
of the centaurs, Actaeon torn to pieces
by a pack of his own dogs.
Actaeon rolls around Kent, burning.
He is lonely, lonely,
for a woman to love him.
How do we call out love?
Do we eat our own shadows?
Make a bonfire of the wilderness in our chests?
Play upon ourselves, drums at every street corner?

Georgie waited outside the Acropolis
kitchen door for the grill princess.
The owner, a short, square woman,
told Georgie whoever he was waiting
for had gone home early.
Georgie Condos presented himself for love,
sitting patiently, hat in hand, toothless, unkissed,
scuffed toe cowboy boots divining the floor.
No love today. No soup today.
No action for Actaeon, antlered hunter.
Georgie doesn't drink anymore
with the centaurs on north Water street.
He's been AA certified for three years,
has climbed all twelve steps.

Georgie can't read the page
or print his name.
His parents turned away
the home school teachers.

His father kept a whiskey dog.
His mother worked hard into gray years.
His grandmother raised him,
taught him never to give up,
to tell the truth plain,
to believe in what the day gives.
Each week he rolls down
to Standing Rock cemetery
to visit her grave and talk
to the cold polished stone
that is her headboard.

Georgie is scholar enough to say
Go screw yourself in good demotic Greek.
Gamos means marriage.
Gamitsou tells you to have a marriage with yourself.
It is nothing you want to do.
It is one of the last islands
before the edge of the world.
You can't live there.
It is all grief and no gravy.

Last night I saw Georgie pump and roll
through the Willow and Main street intersection,
dodging cars, honk, damn, honk.
I'm going to plaster an orange triangle
on his wheelchair back, like an Amish buggy,
and festoon his spokes with reflectors.
Somebody runs over Georgie Condos,
I'll leave town forever.

Cassiopea, abandon your sky chair
and come down to love this tender man,
take him back with you
to live together in *gamos*,
wheeling Georgie through the Zodiac traffic,
both drunk for good on the centaurs' dark wine.

SPIRIT WANDERS BLIND, WANTING WORDS

My good wife spruces me up
for her niece Wendy's wedding,
a new pair of Ecco shoes, Swedish,
ninety three dollars, cushion sole.
I add a yellow shirt with blue stripes,
L.L. Bean, three dollars at the Portland Goodwill.
New 501 Levi's with a baggy butt.
I could shoplift ten pounds of potatoes in these.
At bridal rehearsal dinner,
the wedding, the wedding reception,
I will be trussed like a tuna in a can.

On my left wrist I tie my one adornment,
a silver bracelet I found in Silver City, Idaho,
a small shop going out of business,
a worn red headed woman who coughed her words.
A bracelet with a serpent twisting round
one turquoise egg, another coral egg,
both held in its coil, hunted by time.

The serpent's eyes are inset with turquoise.
She sees every house on my block.
It is from the hand of a Zuni silversmith,
Effie Calavazi, one of her last pieces,
now ninety four years old
and tented in blindness.
She beat silver into this shape,
stole eggs from the sky gods' nest,
the lode of the sleeping mother.

I strap this talisman to my bony wrist,
handcuffed to an unseen world.
I must learn to drink the cactus,
to slow step with the serpent.
At the wedding,
raise fists in celebration
of love's hard march.

OFFENDING THE FAITH

An armless man blocks the trail.
His hair is combed with saliva
and wood ash.
He leads me to the hut
where the barechested man lies.
The ground is burning.
Horses run through the village.
I know, if I do this,
everyone, from now on,
will be fed only water.
A bow. An onyx cross.
A severed finger.

In the highlands,
it is already winter.
I have been climbing
for three days.
An animal skin.
A blackened honeycomb.

In the maze,
the corridors of stone,
when I am still,
there is only sky.
I am lost for good.

WHEN YOU BOIL RICE, KNOW THAT THE WATER IS YOUR OWN LIFE.
        —Zen saying

Pay the bills that matter.
Start with the william who suffers his winters
planting the snowfields with sunflowers.
You owe the one handed woman
who conjured your secret supper
in the big iron wok, stirring
scallions, ginger, noodles and tears.
Beautiful ironwoker, steamfitter,
polesitter, bingomistress, tongwielder.
Your little joy is a dead tree
to which to tie your donkey.
Empty your purse.
Clean out your closets,
all your color skins, your plumes.
The way is not a path.
Lin-chi understood the Buddha
as a privy hole, the bodhisattvas as jailers.
Pay the bill for the water
in which you boil the rice.
The rice sustains the body.
The water. Brew saki, that sour carnival whiskey.
Invite a drunkenness from which you cannot sober.
The iron wok, little ferry boat, slowly spins in the current.
Tumble yourself aboard.
Kiss the palm of the hand that brushes your cheek.
The snowfields lie above you.
Pilgrim, you are going home.

Poem Left for my Daughter Meg to Read as She Walks to School the Morning of her Eighteenth Birthday

Six eighteen in the morning, September 30, 1981.
The birth was hard, your heartbeat irregular.
The doctor cut your mother
and lifted you into the world.
Nine pounds, six ounces.
After the two of you were safe and asleep,
I found the Buckeye bar in Ravenna,
just me and the sunrise bartender,
the place dim and swept.
I have a new daughter, I told him.
Megan Ryan Ragain, a new star in the night sky,
a small lily in the fields of heaven.
He had a whiskey with me and wished us luck.
Luck to you, to Winken, Blinken and Nod
asleep in a trundle bed, fishers four.
I am with you now, adrift on a starry sea,
riding the thin air, measuring
by stars whose names I don't know.
With you now in the wooden shoe.

THE DOOR OF THE WATER HOUSE

After sunset, I am fishing the neck east of the family pier, a shad Rapala lure flipped toward the weed bed. A wake behind the lure, a soft smack. The bass goes down, then comes straight out of the water, shaking his head. He swims at me, goes under the pier, nearly taking the light spinning rod out of my hands. The drag doesn't work. The rod doubles, the tip underwater. Then, he quits, rolling on his side, spent. I lock my thumb in his grated jaw and lift him out arm's length. He shakes himself, heavy, like a wet dog.

Little Brad sprints down the sidewalk, with a whoop, tennis shoes pounding. He wants to hold the fish, too heavy. Brad pats its head, talking to the bass with his small fingers. I tell Brad the fish will die up here in the air; he breathes water. He is hooked cleanly, one treble in the lower jaw. I free him, drop him back into the murk of the lake. He labors to swim, wobbling, gills flared. For a moment, he wanders near the surface as if stupefied by the air world. Then, he sinks out of sight. Six pounds, maybe seven. I tell four year old Brad the bass is going home.

Let's think about him, I say. We sit in silence for a long time. Brad is near shore; I am half way out on the pier. *Majo,* pipes little Brad. *What? I been thinkin bout that fish.* He gives me a sidelong, measured glance as if I am supposed to know what pictures he has been seeing in his head. Little Brad dreams the fish as a scaled brother, a wingless green and silver water god. The bass swimming his sore jaw back to his water house where the minnow children cheer his return and swim figure eights of joy around him. Then the story he'd tell, the balsa deception, the wounding, the leap into the other world, the voices, that thin water named air, the release.

AUCTIONING THE SKYLARK AT A BRADY CAFÉ OPEN POETRY READING

I count among my things
a blue Buick Skylark, born in 1972,
Detroit, Michigan, a two door coupe,
its lines sleeked out along the sides
like the duck's ass haircut I once wore.
Silver blue, Eldorado lodestar,
starship of the fleet,
black vinyl, leather like interior
that always smells factory fresh.
The 350 cubic inch V-8, dual carburetor,
starts right up, warms right up
and idles down into a whum whum
whum deep throated growl,
two barrel music, a top end
of a hundred and ten miles an hour.
I paid fifteen hundred dollars
for it three years ago,
the reluctant seller,
one Rita Fisher, Morris road, Kent,
a retired librarian.
Call her up; she's home.

Tonight, I offer this devil's sweet chariot
to you for 410 dollars.
410, because that was the year
the Visigoths sacked Rome
and this is the year they sacked my house.
410, because that is the gauge
of the shotgun in my closet.
410, because that is what it is worth.
410, and I am about to know you,
through your acceptance of this offer,
your unsullied trust,
the clumsy, homemade wings unstrapped from your back,
grounded, walking up to me,
burning with certitude, your arms open,
to buy and ride this silver blue Skylark,
to be blessed,
to fly.

How to Get the Love You Deserve

The infomercial relationship preacher
instructs the upturned faces,
holding hands.
When it comes to sex,
men are like microwaves,
women like crockpots.
The couples unlink fingers to applaud.

I remember you,
out where the power lines hadn't reached,
a pit of fire,
a whole hog sizzling on a spit.

Jim Harley, the Greek novelist, my friend the man of words, rides in the back seat, Jim Harley, yahoo inventor of worlds, as we cross the Florida everglades on old US route 41, in the budget rent a Ford, Jim Harley, with his Macedonian, the-gods-made-us-do-it grin. We stop at a road-side fruit stand. Jim buys a bag of tomatoes. He wants to eat one right there. You can't stop a Greek from doing what he wants. No running water. No way to wash it. Then, as we are backing out of the dirt driveway, the Hispanic farmer, a slight, curly headed man of forty or so, sprints out to the car with a plastic bottle of water and a handful of nap-kins. Jim washes a couple of tomatoes and eats them on the spot loudly, tough skinned shippers, but no matter. Those are real February ever-glades nightshade tomatoes, like eating red sunlight. Thank you to a man we'll never see again.

This is when I tell Jim I miss the company of farmers. My grandparents on both sides were corn and soybean farmers in southeastern Illinois. So, Jim Harley's question: *What is it about farmers you like?* Humility. I tell him they are humble because they are men caught between the earth and the sky, humble because they are held in a bigness which they can-not make smaller. I can look at a man and know if he's a farmer. *How*, asks Jim. We are rolling along that bare section of old US 41 just outside the Miccosukee reservation, the billboards advertising air boat rides through the everglades and live alligator wrestling. *How? Farmers have meat windows in their foreheads. I can see it.* It is quiet in the back seat. *What do you mean?* It is nothing can I explain. *It's like a beautiful woman naked, mowing your lawn at daybreak or a leprechaun delivering your mail or a UFO levitating a school bus full of cheering kids, or a unicorn drinking at your bird bath. You have to see it. I can tell you about it. But you have to see it for yourself. It's a meat window about the size of a matchbook.*

As a kid, I was marched along to the Olive Branch Methodist church on Higginswitch, with Grandpa and Grandma Totten. I saw dozens of meat windows on any given Sunday, that swath of white skin high on their foreheads where the sun hadn't burned them. Farmers seldom take off their hats. They eat dinner and hump midnight love with their hats on. But, in church, they have to show their meat windows to the heavenly father for it is his gift to them that they might see the work that lies before them and bend to the task. This isn't a third eye or a periscope on a skylight or a contact lens. It is a meat window. And if you don't under-stand me by now, you are not going to get it. Jim's thinking about it. *Is it a metaphor?* No. Jim says the Greeks have a term for talk like this. *Exophrenon. Say it again. What does it mean? Out there, crazy, out of bounds, nuts. Exophrenon.* We both laugh. Both of us could use a window in our thick skulls.

We pull over on a sideroad, get out and pee. An old couple appears out of nowhere, pedaling slowly on their bikes behind me as I stand feet wide looking out over the treetops, making a golden piss snake on the hot asphalt, twisting its way toward the ditch and on into the everglades. We all live downstream. I finish with a shake. The bikers pedal hard and up the road. *You scared em with that thing,* laughs Jim. *They think you are an exophrenon.* We climb in and slam the heavy doors. The everglades are old. Eyes watch us in secret.

The Trail of Garlic Tears Leads Right to My Door

My mother asks me tonight
if I remember when the goat people
came to stay with us, maybe thirty years ago,
how the cross country hippie crew
parked their old rainbow school bus beside the house,
snaked an extension cord through
an open window and plugged into our lives.
The goats wandered the neighborhood,
ate most of it, flower beds, bushes,
leaves as high as they could reach on their hind legs.
Mom said they left after a couple of days,
off to see the wizard or give the devil a haircut.
She couldn't have made it up.
I don't remember anything about them,
though if I did, it is the kind of thing
I'd never let go.

If they were here,
I wonder why I didn't leave with them,
tying a new red bandanna around each goat's neck
and one about my own, raiding midnight gardens,
digging new potatoes and nipping the heads off zinnias,
chomping my way down the clothesline,
saving Victoria's secret for dessert.

I do remember the day
that bucket bosomed, pig tailed
muscle nun from Fort Collins, Colorado, came to visit
and rode half naked on her pet mule across Vernor lake.
That mule paddled head high like a big hairy duck.
Her bosoms would not sink.
The sun could not set.
Neighbors stepped out of their houses
to gawk at the lady and her Loch Ness mule,
that thing from the mountains.
After a few days, she packed up
her mule and her hard, hard candy
and headed north up Illinois route 130.
I heard she rode that mule
across the Sea of Galilee

and later married a garlic farmer in upstate New York.
The last word I got was
they drifted like the frost line
over the Canadian border
and evaporated into thin, cold air.

LAUGH SOLITUDE TO THE BONE
—for Ben Gulyas

Spoony Paine was a son of a bitch,
whipped his kids with a hickory switch.

Spoony Paine walked and talked the streets of Olney, Illinois, my home-town, in the mid 70's. He was one of the last river rats, those solitary men who lived down in the bottoms, half wild, uncurried. Word was Spoony took up lodging in an old school bus, down by the Little Wabash. In the good weather, he'd walk along the tracks, just appear out of the weeds and skulk around town, muttering and cursing to himself, kicking at things that weren't there. Folks knew him as a kind of crazy uncle, a lone survivor crawling out of a bomb crater, a post Apocalypse cockroach man, everything the town tried to chase off, come back, Rumplestiltskin returned to marry your favorite sister and piss in your bird bath. Passersby taunted him with *Hey, Spoony*. He'd shoot a fist in the air and never look up. High school yokels made a game of cursing him back in his own voice, a guttural *god damn... raw rum rumph*. That made him furious. It's a wonder he didn't grab an ankle and tear him-self in two.

The Town Talk cafe, on Whittle avenue, is a block from the Richland county courthouse. Over the noon hour, it was jammed with lawyers, clerks, retired preachers, old ladies with hard hair, Olney's working hoity-toity. In came Spoony, one day, the hungry troll, who pushed his way to a corner table. Nobody wanted him there. Nobody wanted him anywhere. The waitresses ignored him, in his five pairs of socks, funky as old headcheese. Spoony finally grabbed an empty coffee cup and began to bang it on the table, a slow drum beat. And, in a gravely singsong, he demanded, *Bring me some god damned chicken*. Folks began to rustle and leave. He got his chicken, fast. He was unwelcome and didn't have a plug nickel, but he was a ripe man who cried out for what he wanted. The lesson wasn't lost on me. *Bang. Bang.*

The bad winter of 76, Spoony got a job, housesitting while a snowbird couple migrated to Florida. They thought they'd do him a good turn. Spoony was to look after things, fair trade. After Christmas, the pipes froze because Spoony opened the basement doors for the dogs that fol-lowed him around. The sewer backed up. He moved to the kitchen to keep warm, slept by the oven with the door open. By late winter, he never left the kitchen and, to simplify his life, he took to shitting in the

119

pots and pans. When one filled, Spoony'd put on the lid and look for another. The first warm spring day, that river rat walked out the door into the sunshine. The owner hunted Spoony for months, said he'd kick Spoony's ass up between his shoulder blades, tie him and drag him behind a truck. Spoony had a way of going where you couldn't find him.

Last time I ever saw Spoony Paine was in the Red Door tavern, Newton, Illinois. I was sitting at the back table with a beautiful red headed woman, honeysuckle dream of my fading youth, her eyes playing on me, me drinking a bottle of cold beer, glad to the brink of fear. In came Spoony through the back door. He spied me, pulled up a chair and got in my face. I remembered how he got his chicken. I bought him a beer. It still wouldn't make him as happy as I was. He was looking at me with his Jack Elam walleye, then at the woman. Then, he leaned closer and growled, through his gumbo teeth, low, between the two of us. *If I was all boogered up like you, I'd walk in the river and drown.* I hunched down my shoulders, squinted my left eye and, in my best Spoony voice, growled back, *Spoony, you're an old son of a bitch and I hope you live a hundred years.* He grunted, eyed the woman again and asked, *You give me a ride back to Olney?* It was about twenty miles. I told him, *You better start walkin, Pilgrim.* I turned to Mary, then back to him. He had vanished, no other word for it, a spectral gremlin fading into shadow. A few years later, Mary followed. She sleeps in St. Joseph's bone yard.

I never liked Spoony Paine. I wanted him to be alive in the world with me, but not his company. This time I was the guy with the girl and the beer. Whatever happens to him, happens to me. Somedays, I hear his song in my head.

HEARING THE WORDS FOR THE FIRST TIME

The skies are clear
for the first time in a week,
November trees bare limbs now.
A jet trail blurs south to north,
drifting up the window pane,
a line of icy breath.
I grind the coffee beans, crunch and whirr.
The kitchen fills with the broken life
of the black bean.
I pour the hot, bitter welcome cup,
check the *Daily Word*, wedged between
the seashell soap dish and the woven basket,
the morning gospel from Matthew, 28:17-20.

> *When they saw him, they worshipped him;*
> *but some doubted. And Jesus came*
> *and said to them, All authority in heaven*
> *has been given to me…. And remember,*
> *I am with you always, to the end*
> *of the age.*

Barefoot brother Matthew, free me from
every doubt. Come drink a morning cup
with me. You have never tasted coffee
like this along that dead, desert sea.

I open the Cleveland *Plain Dealer*,
today's entries, Thistledown,
the thoroughbred race track.
Read a page of your local phone book.
Then turn to the horses' names.
How pale the names we carry
throughout our lives, tombstone tattoos.
Racing this afternoon at Thistledown:

> *Glimmer of Hope*
> *Whispered Illusion*
> *Raise a Ruckus*
> *Silver Riddle*
> *Secret Mover*

Blue Moon Night
Water Run Deep
Heart Mender
At Sword's Point
Set the Dice
Yukon Due It
Bionic Star
Salt N Water
Hope for Soul

There is no doubt in me, this day.
Give me ten to win on *Hope for Soul*
in the twelfth race, six furlongs.
He breaks from the eleven post
and will be carried wide on the first turn.
This is not a smart bet.
Hope for Soul is not an expectation.
It is a mumbled prayer
in a drifting midnight boat.
It is a willow tree on a river bank,
no taller than a man, its roots
eaten away by floodtides,
leaning toward the dark waters.
Hope for Soul is the river's yearning
for salt as it runs toward the sea.
I lay down another win bet
on a horse named *Salt N Water*
in the fourteenth race, coupling
him with *Lady Lu* in the thirteenth,
a late daily double.
My wife's name is Lu, a woman
who relishes *Salt N Water*, Atlantic,
Pacific, Salt Lake City.
Salty Lu, wade back to me.
Bring the money in a paper bag.

If I Had One Wish

The year I was seven we moved to the old Eaton place at the west edge of Olney, across from the skating rink. A beautiful red haired woman Jackie Jared had lived there before she came down with T.B. and was taken away to the sanitarium. She was a silk tapestry, a Raphaelite, kissed by strange lips, doomed. Before we could move in, the house had to be fumigated with sulphur candles. I can still taste the sulphur, the long pollen trail of smoke.

Next door was the Frisina drive in theater. My window faced the screen, across the acres of speakers. I could lie in my bed, pin back the curtains and watch the movies every night. The outdoor screen was scaffolded like a window in the night, through which I could look as long as I could stay awake, a world that did not take into account my life. The white screen was repainted every summer. In 1947 technicolors were fresh.

I was a cowboy. I was at home on the range in the westerns. One hot summer night Linda Darnell stood up in the Illinois sky, dressed like a gypsy, black hair trussed in ribbons, wearing a watermelon red dress and silver heel boots. Some desperadoes had chased her on horseback into a box canyon. They caught her mount by the reins and for a moment her angry face, eyes flashing, filled the night as she cut at the man with her riding crop. They couldn't have her. She was too much for them, protected by her own fierce nature. Even at seven, I knew they were unworthy of her. I wanted her to love me, skinny peckerwood that I was, wanted her to claim me across the lot of cars, to turn her twenty foot tall face directly at me behind the curtain. I wanted her to tell these scuffy buttholes, through her teeth, her eyes killing all doubt, *You sons a bitches can't have me. My heart belongs to Maj Ragain.* And they'd scatter like curs. She'd turn and smile at me, her nostrils flared like the barrels of a shotgun, and we'd ride off together into the years. After the movie ended and the carloads filed out, I lay my head on the pillow, exhausted by crazy technicolor love.

We moved that fall, my father following the oil fields sprouting around southern Illinois. The Frisina drive in lingered through the 50's, staying afloat with soft porn and bucket of blood popcorn films. The empty screen stood for years after the drive in closed, the lot overrun with weeds, the wooden post stripped of the speakers. Our rundown house was finally bulldozed and burned. I followed Linda Darnell in the movies after I grew up, faithful, knuckleheaded, sleepless, my six shooter under my pillow. I still look for her out the window, summer nights. Sometimes it seems I turned out to be just another son of a bitch in pursuit of her up that blind canyon.

SUMMER OF THE TONGUES

I spent most of the summer of 1946 at my grandparents' farm, south-eastern Illinois. I was six years old, just beginning to wake myself up, to register everything like a thumb print in warm wax. Every Wednesday night and twice on Sundays, they towed me along to the Olive Branch Methodist church where the roll was called up yonder, and we were washed in the blood of the lamb. It was there I first heard one of God's children speak in his tongue, burning with a Pentecostal flame. I could smell singed hair. That night, my Aunt Fanny bolted to her feet, shook all over and pranced down the aisle, her meaty forearms raised to heaven, foam at the mouth, Aunt Fanny rattling like a hip-hop, voodoo machine gun, spit flying, a hair raising stream of ishkabibel. I know the bible calls it a gift from God and I don't understand much, but to me it was all Aunt Fanny running her mouth, crowned by a flower encrusted pill box hat, having her way even with God. My view of Aunt Fanny had by then been colored by a story my mother had told me. When Aunt Fanny wanted to torment her gentle husband Otis, everyone called him Otie, who worked as a B & O railroad repairman, straightening ties, driving spikes, she had her own devilish trick: she would pack rocks in his lunch bucket. Noon came. The men wandered to shade. Each opened his bucket. For Uncle Otie, one day the menu special was igneous, another day metamorphic. In any case, it was a lunch bucket of rocks. After I heard that, I stayed away from Aunt Fanny and her honeysuckle perfume, thank ya Jesus hugs. It became my first benchmark for a mean spirit. Years later, I went to the Richland Memorial hospital to say good-bye to my Uncle Otie. He by then was a small waxen effigy of a man, propped up on pillows, three quarts low, stomach cancer. I shook his thin hand and said, *Get better, Uncle Otie.* The last time I saw him. On the bad days, I carry that lunch bucket of rocks when I go to work on what is broken. Uncle Otie's lost husband lunch bucket is forever shadowed by Aunt Fanny's pillbox Pentecostal baby's breath crown. Rocks are harder — and older — than bones.

At the height of that summer of tongues was the revival, a Pentecostal solstice. The preacher's name I've forgotten — and I don't want to make one up — but his daughter's name I have carried with me these fifty odd years. Fairy. She wore a yellow dress. She was my age. The preacher and his family came for dinner one evening during the weeklong revival. Other members of the Olive Branch congregation brought in food. It was a groaning board, a mountain of fried chicken, piles of mashed potatoes with lava runs of hot butter, a wheelbarrow of green beans laced with bacon and onions, a magic tureen of gravy. The children were ushered off to the front room where card tables were joined. I made sure I sat across from Fairy so I could stare at her each time she looked down at her plate. She didn't eat much. Being a fairy, she didn't have to. She looked as if she ate sunlight or licked the colors off things with her eyes. In a moment of lump in the throat bravado, I asked her if she wanted to see my special place, my treehouse. We slipped out the front screen door, around back, across the chicken yard, to the big, gnarled plum tree which stood sentinel at the center of my kingdom. I had nailed some boards up the trunk to provide a foothold and up maybe eight feet Dad had hammered together a platform. We didn't climb. I wanted to hold her hand, to forge an undying bond between us. Her mother called from the house. The rest of the evening, she stayed close to her father, hardly looking my way. After the pie and the ice cream, the Pentecostal family loaded up in their evangelical station wagon and drove away into the years. If I had known how to write at that moment, I'd have pressed a note into her palm.

Fairy, don't leave me here alone. These aren't my real parents. Take me with you. I don't know whether fairies ever learn to read. No need to. I longed for her to look into my soul and tell me what she saw, to speak to me in that silent tongue. I could have understood.

Years later, a young woman appeared at my door, on the arm of a friend of mine. She was whiskey buzzed, a brown bag pint in her purse, hair tied up in careless black velvet ribbons, a fading love bite on her bare shoulder, early twenties, yellow dress. The three of us sat on the back steps, drank beer in the new summer darkness, talked the humming life of poems, money's dull knife, the argument with the world, the unmapped years to come, what kills the heart, what can't be said or danced. They stumbled down the driveway, warming one another with soft laughter.

The chronology was wrong. Fairy had to be in her early sixties by now.

It was her all right. Time does not count the beats of a fairy's heart.

No fried chicken. No everlasting arms to lean on. Just a handful of dirt. A plum stain. The last light in a tall tree.

GAIL RAY'S DROWNING IN OLNEY POEM

Gail Ray drowned in the heat wave,
August, 1983, her death ruled an accident
by the Richland county coroner,
an epileptic seizure while bathing.
She drowned in the bath tub,
soapy water found in her lungs.

Gail Ray used to throw whiskey ice at me
from down the bar at the South End tavern,
just north of the B & O tracks in Olney, Illinois.
She'd wink and pass me the pancake one more time,
the old grim bally hoo.
Hey skinny man. Where you been? To the North Pole?
You still look like a dog playin in traffic,
tryin' to get hit.
Hey beanpole. You learned to leave it alone yet?
Huh? Well, look at these. You never seen whispercaps
as big as these. Not even in your dreams.
Don't touch 'em.
These were the breasts
between which to hide your secret life,
or to ride out the flood,
kapoked and abob.

Gail Ray was as big as a Frigidaire,
late twenties, hair cut in bangs.
She was married to that dark honkytonk,
the South End. She worked there.
She drank there. Two summers ago
she sped and starved off a hundred pounds.
Her breasts got even bigger
and men got sillier.
No one knew what to do with her,
so they left her alone.
She drove to Texas, lived with a goat roper,
come unglued and was back within a season
at the South End, first stool,
her back to the window, home again.

The night before she drowned on the prairie,

I saw Gail Ray a last time.
She leaned to me, whiskey breath,
mascara wink, and pulled down
the black scoop top to show me
a new tattoo on her left breast,
a rose abloom in three colors,
near the nipple,
one peek, two, not a third,
the elastic snapping shut.
Gail Ray laughed and pointed to
a barechested wild boy at the bar,
stumbling around in one boot,
mud in his hair.
She whispered to me,
Look at him. He walked twenty miles tonight
down from Newton to beg me to marry him
and if it gets dark enough, I just might.

Gail Ray never wanted to go home alone
and she didn't that night
when the bar lights came on.
She had been courted that evening
by the thin man
who had suppered on broth, bile and salt,
the hardkisser pale as bathwater
who stood at the bar's end,
watching her and sharpening
his tiny prick on a whetstone.
He waded into the tub
with Gail Ray that August night,
laid her down,
knee between her breasts,
Gail Ray clutching at the scudded sky.

He is one of a legion of killers
recruited from the realm of the unloved,
the unclean, the unclaimed,
from the realm of the hungry ghosts,
the tormented afterlife of those,
who, in this world, could never get enough.
They are cursed with bellies as big as a furnace
and throats the size of a needle.

This spirit takes his form
from whatever is at hand.
His substance cannot be other
than what we have allowed him.
He cannot come to us except through
our misguided yearning for him.
The seizure is his attempt
at possession, as in the act of love.

That last night I would have seen him,
had I turned to wave goodbye to Gail Ray,
as the door opened on Whittle avenue,
this jigglebellied, naked demon
astraddle her shoulders,
making her the beast with two backs,
spurring her hard
and home to come clean.

Goodnight, snowwoman,
iceboxed heel to head,
turning between the poles.
I ask your blessing.
I have begun to imagine a death
for myself unlike yours.
It has taken the form
of a tiny hummingbird
who will one day eat away
the honeyed life of my brain.
Cage him in your ribs.
Blanch his colors with your new cold.
Fatten him on whiskey ice.
Confound his name.
Gail Ray, keep him from me for a while.

KEEPING THE WINTER ACCOUNT / FEB. 4, 2000

My mother sends me a holiday subscription
to the *Daily Word*, Silent Unity's magazine,
a fresh prayer for every day of the year.
This snowy day, the lesson is forgiveness,
the final fruit of love,
the last banana on the tree of life.
Forgive, and you will be forgiven — Luke 6:37.
I am an elder brother in the silent unity family.
The front door is always open, 1-800-669-7729.

John and I drive through the ice and snow
to Kreigers farm market, past frozen Silver lake,
the gaunt fingers of trees, iron pickets.
John says it must be hard to live
inside the Arctic circle, everything blasted
into white and gray.
Once you saw the colors
you wouldn't go back north.

The Kreiger's lot is an asphalt rink.
I walk in tight little crutch steps,
hung in the air by my shoulders.
I forgive the muckaluck beast
whose only life is in my head.
I want to learn to live on the black ice.
I walk into a forest,
fists of plantains, bunched asparagus,
ginger root men, mountains of thompson grapes,
apple heads brushed with reds and yellows,
blue ball potatoes, dewed lettuce bouquets,
fava beans bagged, heavy hearted daikon radish,
bins of Indian river citrus, mouth harp snap peas,
berries of goose, straw, blue and rasp.
I sack up rouge pears and parsley sprays,
zucchini flashlights and bocce ball grapefruits,
hairy kiwi balls and parsnip spikes.

In the State road paperback exchange,
I find the owner in the back,
dumping books out of grocery bags.

Stacking them in towers of words.
She ties her heavy brown hair
with red ribbons. Her name is Dahlia.
She sells me honey husked Rumi
and silver boned Rilke, half price.
Each is worth a continent, a river, a sky.

The word *humor* stems from the Latin *umor*,
meaning wetness. There is no dry humor.
You are laughing at somthing else.
Umor grows next to *amor*, crazy love
that needs no feet to walk.
Love is always wet.
No such thing as dry love.
You are feeling something else.

My daughter Meg returns from her work,
a hostess at the Ground Round,
a banquet for the KSU track and field team,
forty chairs, $ 5.50 an hour.
She is wearied by commerce, ready for bed.
I wind her guardian angel snow globe
and turn out the lights.
The tinkling music follows me out of her room.
Twas grace that taught my heart to fear
and grace my fears relieved.
I have never understood these words.
I sing them over and over,
to myself, softly, in the darkness.

TRIUMPH OF THE CROSS, A POTATO LITURGY
—On My Sixty Second Birthday

The moon flowers murmur among themselves
outside the bedroom window.
The saucer size white flowers open at nightfall,
big silky lockjaw mouths yawning
at the hidden hours,
drinking the slow breath.
I can't find sleep.

If I could walk,
I'd leave tonight
wading the Cuyahoga river
to its headwaters,
from the dammed, silt choked flatlands,
back to the one spear wound
in the earth, north of Burton,
out of which its clear, untroubled
life flows. Pray till I am empty
and move on, tracking the Mohican river,
the Kokosing, the Walhonding, the Mahoning.
Praise water till I become that,
free of bones, skull and teeth.
Cup me in your hands.
Keep me.

The Japanese celebrate a birthday
with three laughs. The first offered
in gratitude for the passing year.
The second in prayer for the year to come.
The last for clarity, to wipe clean
the mind and heart.
There is another laughter, beyond these,
drunken on the whiskey of headwaters,
praising spirit written on water.

This birthday is swallowed in work,
tearing up the bathroom floor, with two friends,
laying linoleum blocks. We lift the toilet
off its base, pulling the giant's tooth
out of the rotted boards,

the lid down shitter in our arms.
The histories of a hundred sad butts,
chased from the seat, swarm like hornets
about our heads.
We clunk it down in the bathtub,
a big uprooted molar.
Stick a big lighted candle in it.
Let's all sing the lovesick blues.

I threaten Mike and Terry
with a birthday joke, a profane parable,
a bohunk psalm. The question.
What do you get when you cross
a penis and a potato?
A hybrid cross, a genetic marriage,
plighting its own troth.
A penis, tipsy with spring, might well
fall for a potato, a dark eyed redskin,
a firm Idaho baker, a beguiling candied yam.
A potato has too many eyes
to be fooled by a penis, that cyclops,
to be hoodwinked, cockeyed with love.
A potato propagates by its own seed,
don't need nobody, imagines its dark
underground life alone.
No romance here, just the forcing
of one thing into another, against
the evening sky of what we don't know.

What do you get when you cross
a penis and a potato?
Boys, you get a dictator, simple as that.
That is where all the dictators come from,
Hitler, Mussolini, Stalin. You name the rest.
Nothing good ever came of it.

There is another cross here no one will name,
the penis pointing skyward, the potato
nailed square across that member,
a Celtic cross no priest would dare brandish,
no colleen would ever wear round her neck
on a silver chain.

We reseat the crapper on the wax seal,
tighten it down, flush three times, no leaks.
We have repaired the broken,
sewn the rent in the shroud.
We are the bangers.
We are the mash.

O god of second chances and new beginnings,
keeper of the years,
here I am again.

KICK OFF YOUR STRAW SANDALS AND STAY
—An Homage

Yesterday, after my wife LuAnn
drove in from Ohio, eight hundred miles,
to our summer cottage in Provincetown,
hauled a Honda full of belongings,
a forest of dresses on hangers,
red shoes, blue shoes, a window box fan,
pillows and teapots, willow green towels,
two duffle bags and a ten speed bike.
After she had inspected each drawer,
moved the sofa to the east wall,
dining room table to the north,
checked out the shower, inventoried the fridge,
she sank down into the beige, overstuffed chair,
kicked off her sandals, put her bare feet
on the worn hassock, smiled and winked,
How do you like my blue toenails?

You knocked on the right door this time.
I am the one to sing your toenails' electric blue.
They are a sky god's turquoise shimmering
in a cold, high mountain stream.
Mortal spring crackle of the robin's egg shell.
Shade of a koala bear holding his breath
all day, stoned on eucalyptus bud.
The last call color of a drowned man's donuts.
The blowsy blue of the notes a drunken tuba dreams in.
The ten toed, twelve string blues of the delta,
muddy waters up to my chin and rising.
They are the color of my father's eyes
the last time I saw him.

Little blue lamps, Krishna's hot eyes,
light every slow step.
Lead me up out of this darkness,
this long night.
Welcome home.

CHRISTMAS

Bells and hearts ring in a row.
Crèche, holly, mistletoe.
The river overhead runs clear and deep.
The children turn in quilted sleep.
We have no words for what we know
In this season of dark and snow.
Light speaks for us, hung in strings.
A star to follow, a rustle of wings.
God rest you through this coming year.
Cleave to the good. Live without fear.

LET THE DOLPHIN DANCE
—A Note to my daughter Megan Ragain

The cape is rainy and cold,
wind steady out of the northeast.
I was up early, coffee,
working at a poem, a response
to Jessica Damen's painting of her daughter
Rebekah sleeping. Over the child brood
shrouded figures and a ghostly crucifixion,
a Christ drained of blood and light.
Beside the bed a stuffed doll smiles,
wide eyed at nothing.
Rebekah dreams on, wrapped in
a shimmering luminous blanket.
It is always about loving or not loving.
The rest is weeds, vanity, rust, a polished bowl.

I remember you in the yard
outside this Provincetown window,
spangled in the July sun,
a flower climbing toward heaven's gate.
The light is like that in Greece,
knifing shadows, humbling darkness.
The light is Apollo, an activity of spirit.

Salvatore, a writer who lives next door,
just walked in with a steaming bowl
of risotto and striped bass, a gift of the day,
too much for him to eat,
the fish too big, a three footer he caught
yesterday in the Atlantic off Truro.
It is lovely, the taste of this fish
he fought to shore and butchered,
beheaded, hot blood to sand.
I ate its wild life,
the long swim through winter storms above,
the quiet hours in the cold depths
suspended between the moon
and the earth's iron core.

Yesterday I was anointed.

An Episcopal church, here in Provincetown,
built of timbers from the shipyard,
worn and silvered by Atlantic winters,
the outermost church of St. Mary of the Harbor.
After communion at the altar, I rolled in my chair
to the back where a deacon
marked the sign of the cross
on my forehead, her thumb, warm oil.
She lay her hands on my head
and prayed for my soul.
I could not kneel.
I am already humbled,
sitting my days in this tall world.
I came to the father
in the ripeness of my crooked longing.
Hineni, in Hebrew, *I am here.*
I bow my head. *I am here.*
The words of Abraham, long ago,
to the same father.
Anointed I am, though I am not certain
what it means, consecration, accepting
the gift, opening the heart, cutting
a small cross in the forehead that
I not forget. May this wound never heal.
These days I seek bewilderment
and little else.

We close up the little cottage today,
load the car, for the move across town.
On the fridge door, I tape a page sized
photo of Ezra Pound taken at
St. Elizabeth's mental hospital, New Jersey, 1958.
He is standing, hands in pants pockets,
shirt unbuttoned, slight paunch, hairy chest.
His head is thrown back, his mouth open,
as if he is howling, at his jailers,
at his God, at a love whose name has been carried away.
The Cantos can't save him.
Alba is blackened,
the fields of memory burned to ash.
Another might judge that he is singing.
I believe he is howling,

I am here.

Meg, may the light play around you
eight hundred miles to the west.
May this day bless, teach and protect you.

Drowning in Water, Wading in Air
—a last word for Thomas Price

Thomas A. Price drowned in Vernor lake, the old Olney,
Illinois reservoir, a clear Monday evening, May 23, 2000.
The lake fingers nearly a mile east to west, the Fox creek
watershed dammed in 1898 with wagons and teams
of work horses. My family bought a summer cottage here
in 1951. I have swum and fished these waters for fifty years,
this sky overturned. That spring sunset John Reeves and I
were casting for bass off the sand spit, Boatman's point.
We watched as an ambulance followed the blacktop round the north side
of the lake and pulled into a yard of a house near the water.
Several people stood, arms folded, looking down.
The body had been found by three fishermen, the only
other boat on the lake that evening.

The Olney Daily Mail obituary posted that
he had been living in Terre Haute, Indiana,
eighty miles northeast. I believe he came here
by following the rivers, the big muddy Wabash downstream
to Vincennes, the Embarras to Lawrenceville, the Fox to
the Long branch, up the spillway to Vernor lake, in the old
lineage of riverwalkers, men who wade air when they cannot
find water, men who are never at home on earth.
My mother said, *It was a good thing you didn't find him.*
I wish I had. He was wading out to meet us when his body
grew too heavy, the water closing in around him.
Had he reached the boat, we would have hauled him
over the gunnel, old gingerbread brother, and rowed home
under the rouged clouds streaked with oyster gray,
guided by the evening star hung in the back porch window.

MARRIAGE

The Queen of Diamonds reads a star map
in black light. Her lover, Orion, wanders
lost in mountains of cobalt blue ice,
broken sword, belt of three burning stones.
They remember a wedding dance,
a whirl of skirts, clatter of neon bones.

The Pleiades, seven starry sisters, musk
themselves elbow to heel, outcrop
of nipple, belly button lagoon, sweat
drying on the inside of the thigh.
They are saried in silks, garnet,
willow, sunflower. They fear only
the butcher knife and the scuttling scarab.
The moonset pulls them down into
the bare branches of trees.

Each summer solstice sunrise, the Pleiades steal
the great hammer from drowsy Vulcan
and break the constellation which binds them.
For a day, they are with us again,
turning over tombstones in Standing Rock cemetery,
singing in the forgotten language of the first gods,
bare arms linked, drunk on May wine,
dancing in the shining shoes of the dead.

What I Should Have Said to the Forty People Gathered at the Youth Fellowship Coffee House, Presbyterian Church, Kent, Ohio, March 1, 1997.

I have been invited here to read my poems.
I won't read many.
I won't return.
It is hard to stand.
Breath is dear.
When I speak into the microphone,
my voice walks around behind me.
I read them for you.
The poems are the quarrel
over where you begin and I end.
The page is our skin.
The poems are for my children,
Sean and Megan, a way to speak to them.

Tonight, Meg showed me a fist sized bruise
on her shin, softball practice, an infield grounder.
Feel this, she said, tracing the purple yellow Iris
with her finger.
Already, the bone is rebuilding itself.
The world wants her to stay.

To those of you whose faces I cannot see,
out at the edge of the light,
it is you I long for.
Find a way to give me
what is inadmissible to you,
what you can't swallow.
I have been working on a poem for us,
a two seater, a double winged hack,
a kitty hawk dune jumper,
a star stabber
to carry us into the borealis noise.

A Peaceful Heart Has Nothing to Do

Marian,

Tonight after the reading, LuAnn and I drove over to Herring Cove beach to see the last light of the day on the water. The ocean was a gun metal gray beaten into riffles. The sunset had faded into a broad, feathered stroke of tangerine through which ran a band of blue gray, the color of an old bruise. Maybe it was because you'd told me this evening that you were first of all a painter, or perhaps it was my finding out that Robert Motherwell lived at the work center and painted here. Maybe the fall onto the gravel woke me up. Maybe I've been asleep for years. The sunset seemed, for all the world, to be a sky high painting which was dying as we watched. When we got back to the cottage, there in the south hung blood red Mars, closer than it's been in decades, and to the right Antaeres, the giant red star, into whose circumference our entire solar system could fit. Antaeres is at the throat of the constellation Scorpio, the scorpion. The throat. Your lines come back to me, from your poem *breasts' lament* against the surgeon's knife.

> *You hang regret's*
> *black stone death's*
> *dark pearl around*
> *your throat*

I had heard you read those lines only this morning. Tonight, I look up and, for the first time, I understand that Antaeres, a dying red star, an old star, is *death's/dark pearl* round the neck of the scorpion. The scorpion is pursued by Sagittarius the archer. There is no escape from his arrow. The bowman aims at the burning jewel round the scorpion's neck. Even the gods wound one another. Each of us wears something that marks us, a herringbone chain of gold, a tie knotted in a windsor, a circle of barbed wire, a noose of hemp. Death marks us. Beauty marks us also. Death is the mother of beauty. I don't understand this yet. Tonight, when I look up from the sky of your poem into that other sky, I almost get it. The *dark pearl.* The dying star.

May 4, 1970 / A Memory

I first came to Kent on a July morning, 1969, having driven all night from Illinois, hungover, raw, leaving behind the carnival undertow of my youth, hot dreams and crazy love. I first saw the town from route 59, Stow, the cluster of buildings catching the sun. I remember thinking it looked like the photographs of an Italian town reared up in the sky. Years later, when I got to Italy, some of the towns looked, from a distance, like Kent. I was glad to find a river and railroad tracks, a brick train station, water and steel joining this to that. Haymaker parkway was still on the drawing boards. I entered Kent over the old Main street bridge and right onto Water street. Always find a water street. Within a block or two, I came across a young man in a rocking chair, sitting in front of a store, orange and white facade, big letters THE SECOND STORE. His long brown hair hung nearly to the ground off the back of the rocker. He wore an olive drab fatigue jacket and was reading a *Ramparts* magazine up close, his rimless glasses on the tip of his nose. I'll start here, I thought, and introduced myself. The first citizen of Kent to whom I spoke was Mort Krahling. One of the spiritual voices of the place, whose spare and beautiful poems sang the soul of Kent, its mysteries, pointing to that which cannot be seen. He was a man whom Thoreau had in mind when he wrote of poets as the means by which a place comes to contemplate its own nature. I was to know Mort for thirty years till his death in December of 1998. The place came forth to meet me in the guise of Mort.

I was twenty nine years old. I settled into the Allerton apartments at eighty bucks a month and began life as a graduate student. I wasn't much good at it, spent too much time at Walter's bar on Water street, gave my heart away every full moon and took incompletes in my classes. Spring, 1970. Nixon had escalated the Vietnam war with the bombing of Cambodia. There was anger and disappointment. By then, the Vietnam Veterans Against The War had organized in Kent. I remember them stopping the traffic on Main street, in front of the Brady Cafe, a hundred or more of them, marching rag tag, bearded, silent, some amputees, a couple of men rolling wheelchairs, Coxie's army come home. Later that day, the vets held a teach-in at Fred Fuller park, under the big trees, a small encampment of listeners bending to the hard lessons.

May 1, 1970. I was downtown in Walter's bar, drinking Rolling Rock and riding a warm spring Ohio night. Around eleven o'clock, after an NBA finals game on TV, the bars swelled over into the street, blocking traffic.

Someone dumped a trash container and lit a bonfire on the centerline, then another. The Chosen Few, a biker gang from Youngstown, rumbled in. The crowd parted to let them through. They did wheelies back and forth on Water street. I remember the biker they called Pappy — the name in bold yellow on the back of his colors jacket — brown beard, tied back ponytail, a skinny yokum guy who looked older than his years. Pappy took off his floppy hat, sat cross-legged in the middle of the street. As the bikers wheelied by, the riders slam-dunked beer bottles into Pappy's hat. At every dunk — nobody missed — the crowd cheered. I cheered. Blake had it right. *Exuberance is beauty. Energy is eternal delight.* The horses of instruction were in the barn. The tigers of wrath were teaching us their wisdom. It was crazy springtime in a country still young, blood surge, hot youth, a protest against every tight bunghole, against every official hand turning the screws on freedom. It was *one, two, three, four, we don't want your fucking war*, just like they told you. Only louder. And everybody meant it. We were together in an odd, unmistakable brotherhood/sisterhood I have not felt since, as if we'd all been swallowed by the same whale. The state troopers stormed in with white helmets/plexiglass masks and billyclubs. Mort Krahling and I ducked into his junkstore across the street from Walter's. That building is gone now. Mort is gone.

Monday, May 4. A clear, warm spring day, everything in blossom. I woke to an apartment full of people. Maureen Halpin and three friends from Edwardsville, Illinois, had stopped overnight on their way to the Bobby Seale/Black Panther trial on the east coast. I drove up to Satterfield hall. Classes had been canceled. A noon rally had been called on the commons. I began walking toward the commons with my friends Steve Newmann and Jim Hayes, a veteran, when we saw the first white plumes of tear gas and heard the barking of a national guard officer over a bull horn, demanding that the crowd disperse. I knew I couldn't crutch walk away from the tear gas and retreated to Satterfield. It must have been just after noon, when I watched a squad of national guardsmen kneel, lock and load in front of Satterfield. It never occurred to me, nor to anyone else I talked to, that the guard carried live, steel jacketed ammunition. We did not think of ourselves as the enemy, dissidents but not enemy, believing the guard to be on a peacekeeping mission, a civil action against an unarmed citizenry.

Jeff Miller, who was a student of my friend Mike Danko, was shot in the mouth at a distance of several hundred yards. That night I sat with Mike out in his yard, in the rain, as he drank and wept. I drank with him but couldn't find tears. I held him. He would not be consoled. As far as I know, Mike still isn't consoled. Something broke off inside him, like one of those city block sized chunks that shivers loose from an anarctic ice cap and begins to wander the cold seas. Something in Mike broke away and drifts inside him to this day.

I offer not a consolation but an understanding. I know they are not the same. The Buddhists tell me we all have three hearts, linked one to the other, like christmas lights in a series. First is the heart of compassion, then the heart of love, finally the heart of wisdom. They open in that order and no other. Compassion, that heart once opened, prompts the opening of the heart of love and that in turn signals the opening of the heart of wisdom. Meet your rage on the threshing floor of the first heart. No other way. No love, no wisdom, without compassion. That simple. Compassion, from its Greek root, means feeling the viscera of the other. Feeling the spleen, the heart, the guts of the other. The other is whoever is not you. Feel that. Start there. The viscera of the students. The viscera of the guard.

Beyond that conviction, I am lost. At sunset May 4, I left Kent, headed back to Illinois. The national guard had sealed off the town. I drove up to one of the checkpoints, barricades, across route 43, just south of the 261 intersection. A young, ill at ease guardsman checked my driver's license, took down the information on a clipboard and set aside the barricade. As my wife Kathy and I drove through, and I was a shaggy, bearded fella back then, the national guard officer, a lieutenant, gave us the finger, smacking his elbow in his cupped hand for emphasis. I am his other. He is mine. If there is to be peace, he must feel my viscera. I must feel his. I don't know another way.

Thirty years later, spring comes again. I live on the other side of the Cuyahoga river in a small house on a dead end street. I haven't gotten very far. This afternoon, my daughter cut the grass. I weeded the flower bed. Maintenance. Provisional orders. A wooden fence marks where our property ends and the neighbor's begins. Everything is in its place. When I look up, it is all vast emptiness. We name the planets after gods we have never seen. We imagine heaven out there. On the bookshelf in the living room is a Christmas gift from my daughter, a photo of the two of us, her arms round my neck. Meg is beaming. I am baring my teeth neath my mustache. I have always been happier than I look, happier than you think I am. At the top of the photo, Meg has printed, in her small hand, *What is not love is fear.* She said she found it in a book, in a doctor's office. I have puzzled over these words everyday. *What is not love is fear.* Something in me resists this stark, unequivocal proposition, distrusts it as neat sophistry, the kind of glibness which always rankles me. But, these words are Meg's gift to me. She has come a long way to tell me this. What it asks of me seems beyond doing. If it is true, then I have lived much of my life in vague, dull fear, acting out of that.

Today, I receive a letter from Adam Brodsky, along with his poems for the annual Jawbone book. At the close, Adam has included a few lines from the *Rig Veda*, the ancient Hindu text.

> *Two birds, inseparable companions,*
> *are perched on the same tree:*
> *one eats the sweet fruit;*
> *the other looks on without eating.*

Those are the two lovers who complement and complete one another, fullness and modesty, action and reserve. The bird who eats not drinks with love's eyes. There is no other to be found here. There is another meaning in these words, the arrow from the Veda which has traveled so far to find me. One bird, whose name is love, eats the sweet fruit; the other, whose name is fear, looks on without eating. Love and fear are inseparable in this life, as are the self and the other. Each is a witness to the other. The two birds are me and the national guard lieutenant who said screw you with his gesture, thirty years ago. They are the guardsman and the students, the students and the guardsman. *What is not love is fear.* They are inseparable.

Tomorrow, I'll find my way up to the commons to hear the ringing of the bell to commemorate the dead and the wounded. The bell is a voice. Everything in Kent is in blossom. Every blossom is listening.

The Moon Rises from the Basement

My friend Al Bartle has turned
the corner at age sixty two
and mailed in the paperwork
for social security benefits due.
Bush money in the mailbox,
silver dollars in the bucket.

Social security.
Think hard about what that means.
If it is social, it isn't secure.
If it is secure, it can't be social.
Social security is a blind man
catching pennies with a tin cup
out the bung hole of a golden calf.
First you tire, then you retire.
You are broke and then broken.

Al, your only treasure is one
you cannot spend: that hoard
of silver apples you have dreamed
for yourself, little moons that rise
from the basement and circle
the bed as you sleep.
This is what holds you here.

You are the eclipsed sunflower
who seeds himself each hard year,
a frosted corona of pale light.

BELLY LAUGH IN NOAH'S BOAT: A HOMILY

The first day in Provincetown closes up in rain and gray washing in off the Atlantic. The shops are empty. The Portuguese festival flags hang limp across Commercial street, white, green and red. I find Chomo Lama in her Himalayan Handicrafts storefront and make my way though the jungle of handbags, dresses, rolled up rugs, to bow to her behind the counter. She brightens in greeting. We wander in talk, the weather, the children, then somehow to a postcard of the great wheel of life, the spinning lotus, the hoopsnake down the neighborhood hill. Chomo holds up a depiction of the wheel and begins to name each spoke. *Om Mani Padme Aum means more than the jewel in the lotus*, she admonishes. *That phrase is for lazy prayer mumblers.* Chomo turns the wheel. Here is the realm of the hungry ghosts, those who could never get enough in this world. Next door is eighteen hells, not one, but eighteen stations of fiery icebergs, cold bonfires and frozen kisses. *Stop, Chomo, too many hells. Is hell in the mind? Where is mind, Chomo? I can't tell you. Chomo, mind is your laughter. Laughter is prayer, wordless.* Her face lights up. She laughs, bells in the cold rain.

Laughter comes from hurt, from brokenness, says my friend Paul. If you don't hurt, you can't laugh. *There is a secret medicine given only to those who hurt so hard they cannot hope. The hopers would feel slighted if they knew.* Rumi. The hopeful laugh. And we are glad. We are not slighted. Even heaven listens for what makes us laugh. We crack the shell. The nutmeat is sweet, bitter and busy in our mouths. Laughter is akin, cousin, to prayer. It wants heaven.

Three guys die about the same time and arrive together at the pearly gates. St. Peter says, *boys, welcome to heaven where you will enjoy eternity. This is your home now. We live here in harmony. There is but one flaw in this pure diamond land. God in his munificence created too many ducks. And he gave them the gift of quack. Heaven is overrun with ducks, immortal ducks, more on the way. God, for all his omnipotence, cannot curb his eternal annoy - ance at a duck quacking. If one quacks, all the ducks in heaven start up. So, boys*, said St. Peter, *the one rule here is this: don't step on a duck. Get it? The penalty is swift and awful You don't want to know.*

The three new souls stepped lightly through the duck fields, shin deep in mallards and hens. Then, one day, sure enough, one of them steps on a duck. One quack and all heaven is aquack. It goes on for about twenty minutes. St. Peter hunts down and collars the poor fella, handcuffs him to the ugliest woman he'd ever seen and says, *the two of you are joined for all eternity. That is your punishment. I warned you.* After that, the other

149

two fellas were even more careful, shuffling through the duck shit, ever watchful. Then it happened. One of them steps on a duck. Quack, quack, all over paradise. Click went the handcuffs. This guy was man-acled to a women ever uglier that the first. Well, the lone survivor resolved it wouldn't happen to him. He became ever vigilant, shuffling through his days, God's free man. He prospered, fattened on manna, living the good life in his part of heaven.

Then, one day, up walks St. Peter with the most beautiful woman any world had ever seen. He snaps the handcuffs on her wrist and on the wrist of the third fella. *You two are shackled for eternity*, said St. Peter, and walked away. The new prisoner of love was flabbergasted at her beauty, and at his good fortune. *You are the most beautiful woman I've ever seen. What did I do to deserve this*, he asks. The woman looks hard at him, shrugs and says, *I don't know about you but I stepped on a duck...*

Eighteen hells. One heaven. One mind. Brokenness. Prayer. Quack. Laughter. Quack is the duck's laugh. Laughter is a secret medicine given only to those lucky enough to step on heaven's duck. The fella who didn't step on a duck, the thoughtful, trepidatious man, is cursed for eternity, manacled to the beautiful woman whom he doesn't deserve. He is her ugly punishment. She will not forgive him till the last duck is drowned in heaven's pristine pond, belly up.

His only hope is to kick every duck he can get to, filling all of heaven with such a din that God himself smashes the chain with his adamantine nine pound hammer—for only God can undo what he has done—and hurls him from the ramparts. Or he could savor his brokenness and cut loose the laughter, laugh and laugh, not at himself or his dilemma, but at the airy nothing upon which even heaven itself rests.

If the kingdom of heaven is within each of us, you have no worry about where you step. On the other hand are four fingers and a thumb and the good chance that this is heaven, here, where you are, right now. We are dead to the past lives we have led, without memory. Perception itself is unborn. You don't know where your next thought will come from or where it goes. And even this heaven which seems without is probably within mind. You will be manacled to someone or thing, beginning with your own thoughts about freedom, that longing to drift like a cloud across God's blue sky.

This is what we have been promised. Look around you with new eyes. Laugh at the nothing that is everything.

Step on a duck.

MONKEY'S TALE: RING OF LIGHT AROUND THE FOOTBALL

The oil pan in the old white Toyota Corolla
is rusted through, bleeding a trail
of forty weight black tears.
A gut shot buck crashes through the underbrush,
trackers following the blood splotches, gaining ground.
Boyle's junkyard cemetery can't have this one.
I drove this banger to Oregon and back,
across the Medicine Bow range, high summer snow,
across the Badlands, wide eyed and worn.
We'll caulk the hemorrhage
with epoxy and fiberglass patches.
Even the dogs sleeping in the grass
know this won't work, mid February,
pale sun spilling over the asphalt.
This is a wad of bubble gum in the devil's ear,
a sore thumb in a sleeping gorilla's butt.

I give a skinhead guy named Nick
a twenty dollar bill to plug the pan
with the mojo gumbo glue.
I don't crawl under old cars anymore,
don't hide in strangers' closets,
don't bellywalk through drainage pipes.
Nick scrambles out from under the corolla,
says she's fixed, ready for the lost highway.
I want to ride this old japanese rusted
wishbone horse round and round the rodeo
wrecking yard till she dies on the track,
a massive coronary thrombosis deep
in its pistoned life.

A neighbor, stocking cap pulled down
over his ears, Mr. Whiskey Whiskers,
saunters across the yard. *You got
a five eighths crescent wrench?*
No, I tell him. *I got a half inch.*
I can't help him. He can't help me.
This is not about a faceless absolution.

The rest of this tale
goes back thirty years ago
to an all night poker table, Brady Lake, Ohio,
where one eyed, West Virginia Frank
dealt a stud game named
six card son of a bitch.
Nobody was any good at it except Frank.
He must have invented it.
One night it cost me the rent money
and the twenty dollar bill I kept in my left shoe.
When I called his last raise, I looked him square
in his one eye and said, *Well, Frank, it's
just you and me.* Mr. full house son of a bitch
paused about ten seconds, spit tobacco juice
in the Folgers coffee can he kept between his feet
and grunted, *Pretty soon, it's just gonna be me.*

It was a fouled mouthed table.
Every man had his antlers strapped on.
Ornery stories hopped from chair to chair:
a naked lady from Memphis stuck on a doorknob;
Old Blue, the appalachian hound, who hunted down
racoons and buggered em to death so nobody
bothered to carry a gun; a horny sailor
marooned on gorilla island; a near deaf genie
who heard the lucky guy rub the lamp
and wish for a ten inch pianist.

Leave the last word to Frank.
*Boys, no doubt in my mind the most sorry ass
thing I ever seen. You all are lucky you
didn't have to be there. What was it, Frank?
It was years ago, in some guy's garage,
after work, we got his pet monkey drunk
on skunky beer. We stood around for half
an hour and watched that poor horny monkey
try to find a way to fuck a football.*

You can fill in the rest,
how that monkey hankered and humped.
Rolled her over, caught his
banana breath and climbed on again,

beguiled by the leather breasts pumped up
and double nippled, the tiny black belly button.
He could not unlace that white G-string.
Football never once kissed him back.
Monkey poked and joked, promised his tree
top heart. Finally, monkey gave up
and wandered back to his wire cage.
Football was left to its dreams
of splitting goalposts, warm handoffs
and careless fumbles, thrill of the hike,
roar of the beer parka crowd.

It wasn't funny. Nobody laughed.
The table got real quiet, eyes down,
every man trying to work it out for himself.
We all felt like that monkey.
We'd all tried that football,
one way or another.
I am glad I didn't have to see it
with my own two eyes.
I wish I'd never heard the story
or played poker with Frank.

Every now and again, it starts
up in my head, this dumbass parable
of love gone wrong, cupid's sweet
poison arrow stuck and festering,
this ringtailed primate brother
wrestling forever with his heart's desire,
his pebble skinned, can't get no
touchdown love.

DUNKIN DONUT PSALM

My daughter Meg and I pull in at the Stow
Dunkin Donuts this clear fall night.
I cannot pass this place without
buying a sack of yesterday's hard tack.
It has been swallowed by fast food
and pick it up here joints,
always empty, a half circle
of orange vinyl stools, buttless,
cooked coffee awaiting a pour.
When Dunkin Donuts proclaimed
a nationwide ban on smoking,
that cut the throat of this
home away from home.
The AA cigarettes, bible, coffee
crowd moved down to the Country Kitchen.

A Hindu family bought the franchise,
a foothold in the promised land,
with dreams of sweet fried dough,
a madras carnival crowd of coffee laughter.
A tall, regal grandfather, a soft spoken wife,
a restless son with Himalaya eyes.
They work it round the clock.
At the side of the lot squats the family's
sad ass forest green, rusted Cavalier,
one of those beached, humpbacked early 80's models.
Whoever sold them this business
sold them this car, you bet.
I wait in our car while Meg, inside, points out her choices,
mostly blueberry, crullers, a couple of cream filled,
more than we need.
An aproned grandfather sacks them up,
smiles, nods thanks and returns to the back.
Though he cannot see me,
my lips shape the word *namaste* to him,
the Hindu parting and greeting.
Namaste, I honor the light within you.
I make gasho with my hands,
bend forward to acknowledge him,
tip my head so all my troubles

—and his—might spill on the asphalt
and run away to the gutters.

The Hindu book of law, the *Bhagavagita*,
teaches us both no man has a right
to the fruits of his labors.
Nothing belongs to us,
not even our deaths.

May this flour kissed, empty pocket brother
be overrun by a caravan of Presley tour busses
pilgrim bound for Opryland,
donut crazy geezers and spandex hot pants matrons
who clean his shelves of every crumb
and drink themselves drunk and happy
on his tired black coffee.
May they spill out into the lot,
daisychain round that broke dick car
and paint it marigold sun crush orange,
polish the hubcaps like the shield of Perseus,
towchain it to the back of the last bus
and haul this golden family out of here forever.
No more dunkin. No more donut. No more day old.
Sing *namaste*, shut down the ovens.

Namaste, the final countdown of bleached flour.
Namaste, honor the light that shines
through the hole in the last donut.

LOOKING FOR OCTOBER BASEBALL IN THESSALONIKI

The National League playoffs begin tonight
in America. Atlanta versus Pittsburgh.
I am on the wrong side of the world.
I turn on the Greek satellite television
and scan around for Three Rivers stadium.

On channel 32, Thessaloniki is playing
Larissa, Greek basketball, heavy thighed guys
in a half court game on a parquet floor.
The players handle the ball as if
they don't know each other's names.
Everything is done without heat or relish.
I switch around and find, on channel 19,
a John Paul Belmondo movie, in French
with Greek subtitles. He is shooting up
a barroom, a pistol in each hand,
like a big nosed Steve McQueen.
mowing down black gangster pimps.
He takes a bullet in the chest.
His Mexican friend, who bites a thin black cigar,
takes him in his arms and tries to stop
the bleeding with his hands.
The Mexican weeps. John Paul is checking out.

On channel 23, a beautiful square shouldered
Greek woman is reading news copy, right at me.
She wears a daffodil yellow suit top.
I know she is bare from the waist down,
her toenails painted a translucent blue jelly fish color.
Her features are small and crowded,
the mouth thin and busy with her report.
Her eyebrows, each must be a foot long,
bushy black woolyworms promising a long Balkan winter
and keeping the entire T.V. screen warm.
I put my fingertips on the screen.
She stumbles on a word
as I trace her brows,
then touch her neck.

I remember years ago

156

driving out of the Pittsburgh tunnel,
out of the mountain,
Three Rivers stadium sitting like a lighted jewel
on the Monongahala river.
That night the Pirates' Dale Berra, Yogi's kid,
hit a towering foul ball — foul balls always
tower — and it came down at me,
in the good seats ten rows behind third base,
an aspirin down an elevator shaft.
My friend Sam Reale, beside me,
rose to his feet to meet
the fruit of our longing.
When he offered his leather hand
to the ball coming down
out of the darkness — I was right against him,
reaching up myself — Sam made a sound
which overtook him, came through him:
a prolonged shudder and then a whinny,
like a horse shivering in the rain
and casting off the cold.
As the ball got to us, Ted Lyons
reached over and took it to his breast,
the ball with its hot, backward spin,
the bite against the straight line.
He held it in the hollow of the sternum.
It just fit. Everything stopped.
The three of us sat down, went back
inside ourselves and didn't talk to one another.
Dale Berra grounded out.

I remember Sam, more horse than man,
clacking around in his shod feet between the seats,
looking up and calling the ball down to him,
unashamed of the moon whinny drumming
out his horsehide chest,
into mine.

DOING TIME

When I was a first grader at Olney Central school,
I got in a fist fight with my classmate Jimmie Jackson
on the muddy noonhour playground.
Jimmie lived in dirt poor Goosenibble,
south of the B & O tracks.
He wore the same bib overalls everyday,
torn up above both knees, flapping as he walked,
and the same crooked, soda pop teeth.
We stood and windmilled at one another, toe to toe, sobbing.

Nobody got hurt.
A teacher separated us and hauled us off
to the principal's office where we cooled our heels,
sitting shoulder to shoulder on the penitent's bench,
two hard boiled eggs.
We had nothing to fight about.
We just wanted to know what it felt like.

In his late teens, Jimmie was sent off
to the Marion, Illinois penitentiary to press license plates
and straighten what was bent.
I went to college to read books and cipher.
That day on the bench, we were hooligan brothers,
joined at the hip, teeth clenched to face our punishment
from the principal with his hard paddle and bad breath.

Jimmie got mad and stayed that way.
The fist in me began to unclench.
I haven't been able to hold on to anything
since I opened my small palm to the sky.

Feeling the Affection of Those Unknown to Us
—Pablo Neruda

My father was drafted
into the Marine Corps
in 1944, boot camp at Paris island,
then stationed at the base, Quantico, Virginia.
I don't remember him leaving.
He sent home a photograph of himself,
dungarees, shirtless, pith helmet,
down on one knee taking the full thrust
of a bayonet into his chest,
the rifle in the hands of a fellow marine.
Why did that man kill Dad? I asked.
Dad had turned his shoulder away from the camera
so that I could not see the blade enter.
Mom explained it was a trick photo,
that they were playing, practicing
war, getting ready for the Japanese.

I was five the following winter
when we took the Baltimore and Ohio
train from Illinois to Quantico
to be with Dad.
We found a tenement off base,
two rooms, bed sheet divider.
At night, rats scurried about,
dancing on the kitchen table,
lapping bacon grease out of the skillet.
The sidewalks were so mean
mom warned me not to go outside alone.
One cold afternoon, I folded and glued
a paper airplane, my Grumman Hellcat fighter
like those I'd seen on the carrier decks.
Hellcat, Hellcat, I liked to whisper that.
Here comes the *Hellcat, Hellcat.*
I had to see how far it would fly.
Twenty feet down the sidewalk,
it crashed at the feet of a kamikaze thug.
I almost made it to the door
before he caught me.

Mom, Dad and I walked down to the park
along the Potomac river, in the evenings.
I built driftwood creatures on the beach
and hunted them with my bow and arrow.
Mom and Dad sat on the bench, shoulders
touching, and smiled at my adventures.
One night, when the full moon laid down
a broad path of hammered silver on the water,
Dad called it Uncle Wiggley's diamonds.
Uncle Wiggley was a 1940's wise rabbit
Gandalf comic book character, a protector
of children, wire rim glasses perched
on his pink nose. He had unrolled
a shining carpet for children
across that big shitty river
whose headwaters were, I'd imagined,
at the capitol building in D.C.,
where the president lived.
I also got it in my head
that Germany was just on the other side
of the Potomac. *What if the German*
soldiers march across Uncle Wiggley's bridge?
I asked Dad. *They'd never make it*, he said.
They would all drown.

My father often took me
to the barracks with him,
where the men lived and waited for war.
They slept in rows of iron bunks
and wore their names around their necks.
I wasn't supposed to be on the base,
always hiding from the white helmeted MP's.
I became everybody's kid,
a peewee mascot for the whole platoon.
One afternoon, my father introduced me
to Corporal Sword, his real name.
He was sitting on his bunk.
My father walked me up to him
and whispered *shake his hand*.
I could see he was different from the others,
as if he were made of something
fire couldn't burn. Corporal Sword

held the congressional Medal of Honor,
the badge of the warrior.
He had, in Siapan or Iwo Jima
or Okinawa, charged a Japanese
machine gun nest that had the whole platoon
pinned down. How final it sounded,
pinned down, a slow lung crushing death.
The story goes that Corporal Sword, bare chested,
sprang from the foxhole, charged the nest,
zig-zagging, dodging the welter of fire.
He caught the hot barrel
of the machine gun in his bare hands,
using his body as leverage
to overturn it, pinning the enemy
beneath their own weapon.
He killed both men with his Kabar knife.
He suffered terrible burns.
The others saw him as a man
whom death had marked but
couldn't keep, protected by his hex of scars,
the red cross on a white roof.
My father respectfully asked
Corporal Sword to show me the scar
as if he were to lower the veil
shrouding an icon. He refused
with a slow shake of his head.
I still imagine that scar running from
his right arm pit to his left hip,
as wide as a belt, pebbled
like the hide of a football.
I wanted to see it. I still do.
It must have been the last part of him to die.

One snowy afternoon at the barracks,
we played war.
Dad suited me up in full combat gear,
ammo belt, helmet buckled at my chin.
His M-1 rifle was too heavy for me,
so he borrowed a lighter carbine
—he pronounced it a carbean—
from a lieutenant in the platoon
and marched me outside to take a photo

of the little marine, bayonet fixed.
A couple of clicks of the camera
and I dropped the rifle in the snow,
just dropped it. I didn't even pick it up.
For a couple of hours, I sat on a bunk
while Dad took the carbine apart,
cleaned it and reassembled it.
He was pissed.
He didn't say a word.
I still have the photo,
the steel jacket ammo Bonzai boy,
Little Private Sword,
ready to give some American shit to Hirohito.
The silence of the father.
We didn't know the war was nearly over.

The marines, the Jireans, liked to fist fight,
whipping off the web belt and wrapping it
around the hand, cinching it tight.
The damage was done by the embossed USMC
insignia on the solid brass buckle.
I had seen a fight outside the bars,
when a marine got thrown through
a plate glass front window onto the sidewalk
while Mom, Dad and I were out for a stroll.
The other marine burst out
the door and jumped him.
It is the sound I remember:
brass against bone.

On Sundays, we visited Dad's marine buddy,
who lived off base, in the country.
Their kid was a couple of years older,
blond, chunky, big mouth.
That day, the two of us got into it
down by what locals called shit creek.
I hurt him and chased him back to the house,
under the porch, went in after him with my belt.
He was blubbering, crawling
into a dark, cobweb corner.
Our fathers got us apart.
I had, as Dad told me later,

cleaned his plow,
dirty business always.
I had nothing against the kid,
but the country was at war.
Everyone was a soldier.
Uncle Sam pointed his bony finger
right at me.
Hitler and his Nazi henchmen
were gathering just across the Potomac.
Semper Fidelis.

One weekend, Dad, Mom and I took the train
up to Washington, D.C., an hour's ride,
to see what belonged to us.
The Washington Monument. Arlington cemetery.
The Great White House. The Lincoln statue.
In the Ford Theater, I stared at
the pistol that shot Abraham Lincoln.
It looked like a toy.
The noose that strangled Booth hung beside it.
The old man told me that
they built a sidewalk over Booth's grave so that people
would walk on his resting place,
so he would have no peace.
I later found out that wasn't true.

Late that Sunday night,
in the D.C. train station,
as big as the town I was born in,
the old man went to sleep
on a concrete bench.
He just lay down and wouldn't get up.
I hadn't seen him drinking,
but I knew he was drunk.
We shook him, pleaded and cried.
Mom and I couldn't wake him.
The last train back to Quantico left us there.
All night we huddled on the concrete bench.
Nothing moved him. It was not just that he was drunk.
It was not a rejection of us.
There was just a part of him,

like the dark side of a moon,
that never turned toward anyone.

The world's war ended
when the bomb was dropped over Hiroshima,
then Nagasaki, human shadows burned onto sidewalks,
like images on photographic plates,
children charred into black paper locusts,
crumbling at the slightest touch.
Everyone in the little town of Quantico
emptied into the streets, laughing,
hugging one another, beer bottles raised
to the smiling American heavens.
The Japanese surrendered.

PFC Ragain and his family were
honorably discharged back to Illinois.
Dad found work as an apprentice carpenter
with the Illini Builders.
Houses were sprouting up all over Olney.
Beautiful young women with big bellies
tended tall gardens of sunflowers.
Mom took in ironing, the wet steam smell,
hours at the board, smoothing every wrinkle,
singing to Jesus who wandered the garden alone.
My brother Michael Roy was born the following spring.
My Father bought a black 1927 Model A Ford
from a tall balding man with a wooden leg
strapped on his stump.

NEWS OF THE DAY / THE SILVER URN

February 27, lake effect snow,
whiteout, my wife calls from
her car, Mayfield road, her voice
small and weary, space capsule hollow,
headed home.

Fifty miles east, a one hundred car,
truck pile up on I-90, Erie, Pa.,
the Peach street exit, a junk yard
mountain, splintered windshield webs,
beached belugas, ice floe concrete.

Bryan, my next door neighbor, walks over,
through the snow squall,
with a full pot of fresh coffee.
He holds it at arm's length,
a chrome lantern, a hot caffeine
head light, to awaken
the snow bank sleepers,
the buried crocus hearts.

We share the bitter bean,
climb out of the black trough of February,
talk the green road west, cheap gasoline,
mountains, Tucson, horses, finally this line
from Rilke: *One moment your life is a stone
in you, and the next, a star.*
No one ever aspires to become a movie stone
or looks up to say the stones are shining
in the Milky Way.
Brian smiles goodbye, raises the empty silver urn,
closes the door.

I have known myself as a stone
for a long time now.

THANKSGIVING TO MARIA AND CARLOS SILVA
who invited me into their home,
Provincetown, Summer 2001

Thank you for the lobster broken,
steamers sprung open,
mussels wedged with linquica,
potatoes split and boiled,
drizzled with olive oil and vinegar,
bread sopped in paprika broth,
white wine, blood of grape,
spirit of table talk, chairs,
checkered cloth.

Your house is too tall, too stepped.
When I stumbled, you stood beside me,
Maria right, Carlos left, my arms
round you. You walked me up,
across the porch. I was light
on your feet. I am done with being strong,
what I could not do
brought me close to you.

Maria, you unfurled the embroidered
linen from your Portugal, the flag
of this day's heaven, spilling from
your arms across the floor.
Your mother planted the seeds,
gathered the cotton, spun the wheel.
You wove the cloth, worked it into
this field of snow bordered by white
blossoms, this spread for the bed
upon which you and Carlos sleep.
May you be held safe
beneath this mother's shield.

Thanks for the merry children
who sat and cleared the table,
laughing, clanking, clinking,
new light spilling into kitchen dance,
hopping, hoping, stealing father's wine glass,
dodging from his glance.

Carlos, you tell me come stay with us,
in the winter when the tourists
go home and the snow comes,
when the old ones, the Portuguese fishermen,
wander into the streets and visit.
We know one another name by name.
We have room. Maria will cook for you.
We will sit at this table, drink wine
and talk into the long night, toward spring.

We break Jonah's body with our bread.
The soup spoon is a viking oar,
the clam shell an archangel's ear.
The food we eat, the work we do,
calls us closer, each
hand on my shoulder,
each fork song on my plate.

THE FLOWER IS A MUSCLE OF COLOR

The moon is waxing.
The cars are asleep
against the snowy curbs.
I stuff envelopes
with seed packs,
outward bound
in the morning mail.
Flower seeds to old addresses,
loves with new names,
friends who live where the air is thin.
Flower seeds, fifty nine cents a hot pocket,
the procreative urge,
the explosion into bloom,
the endless quarrel with winter,
the bulletproof vest of the trumpet vine,
the shotgun shells of an early spring.

I am not a man
who rents a Jupiter missile
and sends his ashes into
the cold meat lockers of space.
I give you bachelor buttons,
perked, rayed medallions in cornflower blue,
the broad, eyelash petals of the cosmos,
the cut throat of the nasturtium,
the zinnia's splintered racket.
I pester you with my offerings,
with what is yet to be.

I send you the letter bomb of forget me nots.
They bloom all season long.
You must burn water.
Sow in full sun.

LAMENT FOR STELLA GIBSON

The seventies in southeastern Illinois
were recession times. The oil fields had dried up.
The Roadmaster bicycle factory had broken
the union, gone bottom dollar.
The Walmart cathedral of tomorrow was on the drawing board,
its gridded parking acres still soybeans.
Lots of folks in Olney, my hometown, signed up down
on Boone street, the unemployment office.
The only work I could find was at the local
radio station, two dollars an hour,
newsman, music man, trashman, third class
radio engineer, on the air from six til eleven every night.
Just me and the three blinking red lights on the tower.

The music play list was soft contemporary
middle of the road bonehead oatmeal for the ear.
Sundown come and the phone would begin to ring.
Requests, complaints, questions, rants, offers of love.
Calls from pissed off, hormone humped
teenagers who demanded Black Sabbath heavy metal or else,
from warehouse fork lift truck drivers craving Elvis,
from Joe Smith, the coin collecting barber who
never told me the same gorilla joke twice,
from a waitress at the Red Rooster truck stop
who couldn't make it through the night
without a Kenny Rogers love song.
I'd hear from half-in-the-bag housewives
who wanted their hearts jumpstarted by Barry Manilow.
Every night I'd get a phone call or two
from Stella, Stella Gibson.
Hello, this is WVLN WSEI fm.
Hello, honey, I couldn't live without you
playing this music, keeping me company,
talking to me in the dark.

Stella was in her late seventies,
long time blind, living alone
in a poor neighborhood dubbed Goosenibble,
down by the Baltimore and Ohio tracks.
One night after the sign off news,

169

and I'd shut down the transmitter,
the phone rang. It was Stella again.
Honey, I am lonesome tonight.
I sure wish I had me a cold beer
and some company.
What kind of beer you like, Stella?
I like them tall boys, nice and cold.

An hour later, I knocked on her screen door.
Stella appeared, flowered housecoat,
hair tied back with a scarf, small shoulders.
I want to see what you look like, she said
and took my face in her hands,
thumbs along cheekbones and brow,
down the nose, lips, chin , dimple.
When she had me in her head,
she led me to her kitchen table.
We split the six pack
as she told me stories about her cats,
her dead husbands, her no good hillbilly neighbors,
her rag rug business.
She made jumble colored rag rugs
and sold them on the radio station's call in
morning show *Quiz n' Tell.*
After her third beer, she loaded me down
with five rugs and kissed me a midnight goodbye,
a quick, squeegie smack at the side of the mouth.
Honey, she said, *Don't you be expecting*
to come around here every night.
One foot out the door, an armful of rugs,
I turned back to her.
Your name, Stella, it means star.

I never saw her again,
though a couple of times, I did leave
a six pack of Pabst blue ribbon on her doorstep.
I quit the ghost voice business
that November, packed my Impala
oil burner and wandered east,
following rivers, sleeping in truck stop lots.
A few years later, a hometown fella
told me Stella Gibson had passed on.

You know she didn't make those rugs.
They come from Guatemala.
She had them shipped down from Chicago.
I know that guy. He doesn't believe in much.

She is in her dark kitchen tonight,
sipping the foam of a tall boy,
singing along with the radio.
Her sure fingers weave the thin rag strips,
pulling the colors through.

I was the nightman.
She was a star.

A Coat of Many Colors

The Joseph's Coat rose, at the northwest corner of the garage, has begun the climb into its second spring. Its blossom is a motley pattern of yellow and red, ascendant, pulling the earth with it. I hear Dolly Parton's clear trill in my head, singing the song she wrote about a coat her mother had sewn of patches, *that coat of many colors my mama made for me*, as an emblem of her love. Dolly Parton. I turn her name over with my tongue, tasting its fruit, its erotic slake, the roundness of the vowels, the upstart double *"ll."* She is the doll of my convict midsummer night's dream, my prayer for a pardon. No sad old padre walking me to the gallows, but Dolly tucking me safe between her whispercaps and carrying me away like the babe I have never ceased to be. Dolly taking me in her arms like a circle round the sun, don't you do me darlin' like that easy rider done. I see her as she was when I met her, early 1970's, living inside a black and white RCA TV dollhouse with Porter Waggoner, her beehive hair, her honeyed bosom, her giggled squeal. I could never fathom what she fancied in that hillbilly bohunk, his basset hound face and lacquered, vertical coif. He sang one song ten different ways. It must have been his coat of many colors: aquamarine with padded gangster shoulders, on the back an orange sun rising out of red mountains, green cactus, a rearing black stallion, the whole scene cobwebbed with silver and studded with hundreds of rhinestone eyes. He was Dolly's Grand Old Opry peacock. She rode his spangled tailfeathers. He couldn't keep her. Dolly folded her hands in sweet prayerful goodbye and on to DollyWorld. Last week, I saw Porter still on the Opry, sporting a new low riser, less is more hairdo, solo in shirt sleeves.

Joseph was the last of Jacob's sons, the fruit of his old age. As proof of his love, Jacob made for him a beautiful coat. After he wore the coat, Joseph began to dream. The sun, the moon, the stars visited his room. His brothers, in their envy, stripped him of his coat and cast him into a pit, conspiring to sell him into slavery, into Egypt. To hide their guilt, they dipped his coat in goat's blood and brought it to their father as evidence Joseph had been killed by a wild animal. The coat was mottled with dried blood. Jacob refused to be comforted. His words were, *I will go down into the grave unto my son mourning.* One of the rose buds is nearly open, a hint of red and a slash of yellow, as if the bud had been dipped in new blood. Joseph sits, his bare back against the pit wall, listening for his brothers' return.

JOHNNY RED KERR/CHIEF ILLINIWECK

WGN, Chicago Bulls basketball.
The coaxial cable stretches
all the way to my house, three hundred miles south.
Johnny Red Kerr's face fills the screen,
the play by play man for the Bulls.
He talks to me as if he knows
I am listening.

Forty years ago, I watched him,
along with the other little warriors,
battle inside a snowy Motorola box.
Red Kerr was the center for
the University of Illinois Illini,
a gangled six feet nine inches,
with a soft hook shot from the paint.
It was, in a biblical sense, unstoppable.
In the 1950's, six feet nine was about
as high as men climbed.
He was not a technician of the sacred.
He was a red headed man with a hook shot.
May I never confuse the two.

After my folks had turned in for the night,
I'd crank the rooftop antenna round
toward WCIA, Champaign-Urbana,
and find the Illini, from the Indian
hileni, the human beings.
At half time, Chief Illiniweck, the team mascot,
a white student from my hometown, in full headdress,
war danced the length of the court,
whooping for the scalps of the hawkeyes,
the hoosiers, the boilermakers.
Red Kerr was the man.
They'd work the ball into the low post.
Red would back in and put it up
with one long sweep of his wing.
On to the NBA, nine hundred
and forty some straight games.
He was known as the Ironman.
He would not quit.

He is a fat man now,
freckled and mottled the way
old red headed post up guys get.

By 1832, the remaining tribes
of the Illini nation, the Kaskaskia,
Peoria, Cahokia, Tamoroa and Michigamea,
dwindled to three hundred people.
By treaty, they gave up their Illinois lands
in exchange for a reservation in northeastern Kansas.

No full blooded Illini is now alive.

DRIVING CAPE COD, THAT SKINNY FINGER

The last hours of spring,
I drive my old Nova all over Provincetown,
down Commercial street,
across Shankpainter road,
out to the beaches, the rolling miles
a protest against my stone feet,
the slow, wobbling steps.

I stop at Bonnie's pies
for a cappuccino and a yellow
poppy seed scone. I ask the
counter man to carry them
out to the car for me.
No reason I can't. He holds
the car door. It closes and catches
my heel. *I got it,* I say.

Herring Cove beach,
a half dozen cars, gray, sixties,
cold wind. I park next
to a gray traveler who has backed
his twenty foot camper
against a curb. He is alone, poking at
one hamburger, one wiener,
on a little grill beside his rear wheel.
He looks married. I wonder where
she is, run off, napping in the camper,
sleeping underground.

The Atlantic is ruffled silver.
Two fishermen, a hundred feet apart,
cast live sand eels for sunset striped bass.
Along the horizon, across the water, I can make out
the shores of Plymouth, twenty miles away.
The whale watching boats — two of them —
cut toward the safety of Provincetown Harbor.
Did the right whale kiss the wrong lady?
A radio voice inside the dashboard tells me
John Lee Hooker is dead at eighty three.

Back in Provincetown, I find a parking space
on Ryder street, near fisherman's wharf,
across from the Café Maria. In front of the car,
a covey of barely teens is farting around,
giggle and grab, pull and pucker.
A big homely dufus picks up a slender, hipless girl
and twirls her around on his shoulder,
WWF bubblegum passion. She screams.
He growls. Then sets her down. She staggers.
Everyone laughs. *That's not funny*, she gripes.
These kids have played here every evening,
swimming in one another's breath,
while the tourists trudge wooden faces
to the ferries, dragging weekend luggage
on little black wheels.

At the Café Maria, a beautiful Portuguese woman
comes to the walk up window to ask me,
Can I help you? I don't think she can,
so I order the day's last coffee in a cup.

In the harbor, the boats are held taut at anchor in the west wind.
A tall man in a red sweater
ties his black retriever to the light post.

Sunday marks the bishop's annual blessing of the fleet.
Bless me, father, in my little boat.

Learn to Wake Yourself with Quiet

In the darkness, the last night of summer,
back porch trellis, a white moonflower
has opened, saucer sized, first of the year.
I come out at noon to mark the twelve fifty p.m. tilt
into fall, solstice coffee, bare feet, counting
away the broken months.
The flower is in the shade, still fully opened,
facing east where this night's waning moon
will rise.

As the day deepens toward dusk,
the blossom begins to crinkle.
The smooth skin of the cupped petals
folds in on itself, a grandmother's mouth
pursing into scorn.

I remember white cotton panties
knotted into blossom on your doorknob,
that flower, door ajar.

I Was Sleeping, But My Heart Was Awake

My son Sean got married today,
in Canby, Oregon, to Kim Anderson,
who was born in this town.
The Willamette valley, everything grows here,
a swath of rich humus,
lava rock dinosaur bone crumble.
The breath of the Pacific is just over the hill,
mile after mile of vineyards.
The pinot noir flares,
camellias and gladiolas by the acre,
macadamia nuts and bing cherries.
The two of them stood and pledged
their love in a small chapel on fourth street.
Sean planted himself tall and straight,
kissed by sweat.
I will, he said.
I believe him.

Love is a sea without bottom.
Its shore is bounded.
Its bays and ports are named.
Everyone who loves deeply suspects
there is no measure to the depth.
The heart is a bathysphere
lowered into those warm waters
which turn colder, darker,
in the descent from camellias
to anemones, to pale squid,
to the midnight mucous tear
that drifts at a thousand feet.

A Respect for the Ordinary
—a farewell to Jack Purdy

Jack Purdy was born and died
in the little farm, crude oil town
Cisne, Illinois, population six hundred and fifty,
reclined in his old Morris chair,
attended by his console cable TV.
He was the mailman home from the route,
alone, roads closed, one leg extended,
the other bent, hands folded on his stomach,
head back, heart caught in midbeat.
He did not want his wife Lois,
life long Lois from Big Thicket, Texas, to find him dead.
She was asleep in a hospital bed in Flora,
a half hour away, when Jack called down
the mercies of death in his seventy-fifth year.
His nephew pried open a window the next morning
and found him, postmarked, a clean getaway.

Jack Purdy was a student of order
who put things where they belonged
and expected them to stay there.
We fished together on Vernor lake
in a small jon boat, working
the weed edge for late summer bass.
His tackle box was neatly arranged,
row by row, mail slot by slot,
every hook sharpened.
Death dumped the tackle box
into the midnight canyon,
kicked in the hull of morning's bright boat.

I asked Lois for a fishing lure of Jack's.
She gave me a three-inch black plastic worm,
white stripe the length of its back,
threaded on a gold hook, a facsimile,
deception, mojo, little mimetic trickster,
an ornament for last year's sunken Christmas tree,
left with me here on the other side
of this river named bottom mouth,
finned night.

Lois sent me one of his coffee cups,
white, cracked enamel, red script,
Campbell's tomato soup can copy,
cheery mug to comfort winter's children,
tomato broth mustaches, apple cheeks,
Jack's morning cup, microwaved five a.m.
instant starter coffee, ignition brew,
dawn beans, ventricular gunpowder,
sunrise waltz.
Jack drank his coffee on his feet,
greeting the birds at the feeder,
the trees, the clouds, the new day.

In World War II,
Jack was a twenty-year-old farm boy courier,
U.S. Army, carrying classified messages behind German lines,
eating the paper after memorizing the words,
a swallower of fatal secrets,
promised torture if he were caught by the Nazis.
His letters back to Cisne
confessed to Lois all he wanted was to survive
and come home to her, Lois Simpson Purdy,
to whom he was married fifty-six years.

His obituary posted at the Hosselton
funeral home remarks he was of
the Catholic faith. I don't remember
Jack as fearing either God or devil.
Nor was he devout.
Rather he gave himself to building a world
in his basement, that bunker.
He found forms in which to house spirit.
Woodworker, timekeeper, clocks
carved from the walnut tree Jack
and his father felled, a rocking cradle,
a dollhouse for his granddaughter. He crafted
a family of reindeer grazing the frontyard snowfield.
He was a fixit man. Neighbors knocked on
his door holding dead toasters, busted
blenders, radios that wouldn't talk.
Jack husbanded a greenhouse downstairs

under the growlight sun, grafting odd
to even, pear to plum, grape to celery,
married Burpee to Bazooka, fathered
a basketball hybrid mutant tomato
that refused death by snow and ice.
Jack had to kill it with a shovel.

The Chinese masters teach
there are only two questions:
when to be firm, when to yield.
Get that right and hold the world in your arms.
For the Cisne mailman,
the secret message was simpler:
just get up and do something, his advice to everyone.
The last time I shook his thick, freckled hand,
he told me to get up and do something.
He never said what.
I don't think he knew.

I drink a morning cup to Jack Purdy.
I cast into the dark waters
whose depth we cannot plumb.
Jack Purdy is gone,
his ashes shelved in the Cisne basement
till that bright morning
his and Lois' bone ember and ash
are strewn together at Johnsonville lake
whose roads they walked so many years,
the scattering beyond record,
up and gone.

There are a Hundred Ways

In the spring of 1952, mom and dad, my little brother Michael and I moved a few miles up route 130 to West Liberty, Illinois, into a big two story house, surrounded by corn and soybeans, trees and flowers. Dad tried to stop his wandering from oil field to oil field, roughnecking they called it, and settle down as the foreman at Eberhart's, one of America's biggest chicken farms, fifty acres of what looked like a public housing project, row after row, only smaller and chockfull of white plymouth rock hens. For the old man, it was the year of chicken shit. He couldn't stick it out. He was the wrong guy for such work. Mom was happy with the flower beds, washer and dryer, a real basement with knotty pine paneling, a garage, Kentucky blue grass to the edges of the fields. I was ten, recovering from the withering fever of polio three years earlier, learning to stalk about on crutches, in leg braces and a back brace, suited up for the battle with the world.

I spent whole days at my second story bedroom window. From it, I could see all the way south over the fields to the blacktop Dundas road. And I could just pick out Richland county's one claim to fame, the five foot tall concrete obelisk — I didn't know the word then — marking the exact center of the population for the entire United States. Governor Adlai Stevenson had came to dedicate it. I caught a glimpse of his bald head in the back seat of a long, black car. I never understood what a population center meant. Dad said it was statistical and it would continue to move westward because that is where Americans were going. Statistical, not a real place, but there it sat, concrete with a brass commemorative plate. Like a belly button, it held the forty eight states together. By 1960, the designated population control had relocated to the west side of Illinois. A couple of years later, an enterprising farmer dug up the historical West Liberty marker with a backhoe, carted it off and planted the field with corn. You can't stop a farmer in springtime. I believe the population center is now somewhere in Iowa, headed for Nebraska. Stevenson lost the presidential race to Ike. It wasn't close.

That was the year I began to dream nimbly over the fences, tree top to tree top, the crest of one wave to another. I spent months at sea, then drifted among the unnamed fjords I'd seen in *National Geographic*, the booming gray silences. I was a peewee hunter, dressed in skins, great booted, my brow crossed with hot blood. I kept steps with the beat of my ungoverned heart. When winter swept over the farmland and I was home from my wanderings, I loved to keep watch out over the desolate fields, the broken corn stalks, the new snow on the headstone. I was forced to abandon my crows nest, my lookout post. We packed up and moved on, another statistic shifting the balance.

One night we drove down to Olney, the Arcadia theater, Michael and I in the back of the 48 Hudson, mom and dad silent in the front. The Arcadia was proud to present a Hollywood blockbuster: *David and Bathsheba* starring Susan Hayward and Tyrone Power. I knew them both from mom's movie magazines: *Silver Screen* and *Photoplay*. The male lead was of little interest to me, a wetcombed, arched eyebrow dandy whose real name was, I figured, a long way from Tyrone Power. I'd already found out from the magazines that smooth move Cary Grant was actually Archie Leach and Judy Garland — that necklace of flowers — was sure enough Frances Gumm. It was Susan Hayward I wanted to see on the big screen in the hushed darkness, playing the part of seductress Bathsheba who brought down the house of the wise, God fearing David. I'd seen her in the magazine photos, doe eyes burning technicolor, tawny hair heaped in ringlets, her belly button deep enough for David to drown in, harp in hand.

That night I wasn't wearing my leg braces and leather back brace. Sometimes I was too sore to do so. I rode on Dad's back. He'd bend down, put his arms behind my knees. I'd hold on round his neck, my fingers bent and cinched in a grip he'd learned in the Marine Corps and taught me. Dad would straighten, shifting my weight till it was comfortable for both of us. Then, we'd walk. I could feel his every step in my bones, the balls of his feet, his high arch — he'd gone to the state meet as a quarter miler in high school — the surety of the heel, the spring. When I rode on his back, I was a head taller than his five ten, a mahoot, a jockey, a surveyor of worlds, grateful in my height, above the struggle of my own halting steps. It was Saturday night so we had to park a couple of blocks from the theater. I rode dad in the cool autumn darkness to and under the marquee, its cavalcade of buzzing white lights. Mom got the tickets. In the full mirrors that ran the length of the lobby, I wondered at the man with two heads, the creature everyone else saw, and realized, for the first time, that it was Dad's fierce warrior's mask which parted the way for us. It was the only time he showed the world that face. I never met the stares with my eyes. I still don't. I was glad for the safety, that little island in the air, the pleasure of our gait, my heart against my father's, in step.

The movie I've forgotten, though I can close my eyes and see, fifty years later, Susan Hayward in that desert tent, lounging on a dais, lowdown and lubricious. I rode out on Dad's back. We took the side exit onto the dark street, mom and little Michael tagging along. We drove back to West Liberty, the bright pictures busy in our heads. Michael was to die in 1965, eighteen years old, a mile north of the house in West Liberty. A car ran him off route 130, down into the ditch, into a culvert, crushing his chest on the steering wheel. Grief entered my mom and never left.

I can't remember the last time I rode on my pop's back. I got stronger and stayed on my feet. I do remember the last time we walked together. It was 1989, the year before he died of a massive stroke in his kitchen. I was visiting him, in January, Seminole, Florida, his little tinted glass window house, 11058 Freedom Way Drive. He lived there with his champagne poodle Rusty. Dad was in the last stages of emphysema, a camel filter in one hand, an albuterol inhaler in the other. His ribcage had expanded as his lungs diminished. He drank air in big gulps. That day, he wanted to take me to lunch, to go in, as he put it. Dad shaved, buttoned himself in a rayon gulf coast shirt, stepped into a pair of checked old-man-to-the-grocery pants, slipped on leather moccasins and announced *saddle up*. I'd never seen Dad on a horse. He used to say it when he knelt down for me to get up on his back. He said it to everyone when we were getting ready to leave. *Saddle up.* I believe Dad learned it from James Arness, that no-trouble-in-my-town sheriff on the TV show Gunsmoke. We never missed an episode on Saturday nights. *Saddle up.*

We drove to Leverocks, a seafood house over by the causeway, one of those Florida restaurants that features senior early bird specials. As we walked in from the lot, me swinging on my crutches, the old man shuffling, for the first time in my life I had to wait for him. He couldn't keep up. The sound of moccasin leather shuffling on the bricks, those short difficult steps, was a rasp of breath behind me, calling me. I held the door for him. He didn't eat much. We watched the fishing boats on the canal and talked about the Tampa Bay Buccaneers, their quarterback problems. He didn't care about much by then. When I left for the airport, I embraced the big, boney cage of his chest. I never saw him again.

I signed the papers to have him cremated in a black vinyl zip up flight bag. The attendants fed him to the fire. The next day, they gave him back to me, a cardboard box a foot square. The heft of it was puzzling, six or seven pounds. The distillation of a life, residue of bone and heart. The crematorium headmistress handed me a small envelope containing Dad's two rings. *Where's his watch? He always wore a watch.* I remember it: worn silver on a red and green nylon band. *We don't have it. It didn't come in with him.* Somewhere a paramedic is counting the hours on my old man's watch. If you read this, give it back. I packed the box of ashes in a small shoulder bag. When I got to Tampa International airport and sent them down the checkpoint conveyor belt, all hell broke loose. Alarms. Security. *What have you got in there?* The x-ray screen showed an unidentified black mass of suspicious density. A bomb? *No, that's my old man.* I produced the death certificate. Guns were holstered. We were waved through. Pop would have loved it. He never found much security in security. I brought his ashes back to Illinois and strew them in the Embarras river, as he wished, out of three Folger's coffee cans, off a bridge a few miles east of West Liberty.

The year after he died, one rainy fall night, I was sleeping, my head near the open window drifting in and out of dream, when Dad spoke to me, at the window. My name, with a certain kind but pointed urgency. *Maj,* a clear, unmistakable bell. I sat up and looked out the window into the rainy street below. Though disembodied, it was his voice, calling me to awaken or perhaps to dream more deeply. A single word, a certitude that we are watched by eyes unseen, held in hearts that no longer beat. Then, last summer, I lay for five days in the intensive care unit, Richland Memorial hospital, my hometown, Olney, Illinois, bagged by pneumonia, half in shadow. One night, my son Sean, called from Oregon. I heard the clear, hardwood strength in his voice, telling me to hold on. I hung up and wept, a big wash of gladness and loss. My daughter Megan called from Ohio, her small loving voice. More tears, sobs, as if I were coughing up ghosts, the wreckage of broken armor. I hadn't wept like that in years. I got quiet, empty up on my elbows in the half dark of the room. At the head of the bed, there was a rustle of light, a white curtain stirring in another world's wind, a shimmer, a parting, to the left, moving, then gone. At that moment, I knew my father was there. It was his breath, its old meaning as spirit, which stirred the curtain between our worlds. It was the kind of recognition love engenders and thrusts upon us. A rustle, a shift of light, no face, no voice, no heartbeat against mine, no broad back upon which to ride. But it was Pop, surety that the body is more than raiment, the life more than meat. It was the tears that melted the ice armor in which I clank about. And Pop found me. I pray for a thunderstorm of my own tears, a drenching, a floodtide. May I drown over and over. Be delivered shivering to a small isle under a clearing morning sky.

These days I have been forcing myself to ride in a wheelchair. It has been against the grain of what I have tried to do for fifty years, to stay on my feet. But, my legs won't work anymore. My balance is gone. My left foot flops like a fish. I have been practicing this submission to being wheeled about. My good wife Lu and I in the evenings fold up the wheelchair between the car seats, drive down to the paved bike and hike trail at Munroe Falls. I get in the chair and we roll for miles, Lu's breath at my ear, passing the wild growth of late August, trying to empty myself into the world that I may be filled. I am learning to meet the eyes of the huffing joggers, the gray couples with their little dogs, the summer struck lovers, the whirring wheeled skaters, the taciturn fisherman. There are those eyes I cannot meet, the shing of the bicycle bell passing from behind on the left, the hard pound of the patterned soles overtaking us, the sweet tumble of the Cuyahoga river which rolls without wheels, walks without feet. The Greeks, in their exuberance and old sense of necessity, have a phrase for it, for what I am learning. *Horevo Kathestos*. It means dancing sitting down. It has nothing to do with the movement of the body. It is an activity of the spirit, how the sail comes to know the wind when it is torn from the mast, how the sailor understands the ocean through the rocking of the boat. When you see me, I'll be in the boat, here inside the barrier reef with you, but it is the ocean I want, the great depths curtained with pale sunlight. *Horevo Kathestos*. A man in a chariot, without a horse. A man in a boat stitched of skins. A boy riding the back of his father, arms cinched round his neck.

ORPHEUS, KITE, AUREOLE, WHALE

Our first morning back in Provincetown, my wife Lu wakes early, walks down to Joe Coffee on Commercial street to bring back steaming cups of the good stuff, the wrenched roasted bean, and glazed cinnamon rolls with pecans. I wake long enough to get up on my elbows for breakfast before falling back down an elevator shaft of technicolor Cape Cod dreams, a childhood mosaic of muddy rivers, wet kisses, an orchard of baseballs. By noon, I have slept away the eight hundred mile road kinks, the short breath, the socket and ratchet of old bones. We roll down to Café Maria, near the wharf. Maria runs out from behind the counter to throw her arms around me. *I been thinkin' about you.* All my life this is what I have wanted, to slip like a ghost ship from my moorings, from this bent body, to become a thought held in the mind of another. Be thinkin' about me. I'll be thinkin' about you. Maria got working hard beauty, not wanting to be this way or that, the beauty of beauty not considering itself, just working in the world with humility and trust without calling it that.

Next to the Café Maria is a kite shop, just at the edge of the harbor beach. Everyday the owners stake out the dozen or so kites in the shore breeze. I am watching one kite, a series of six bowl shaped wind socks,- the largest helmet sized, the smallest cupped hands-all tethered to a pole, six hats in a row for the northeast breeze, blue, red, yellow. Streamers finger out from the bottom of each. I gather it in for a long time. Something in me lightens, rises up to meet the kite playing in the wind. It is a wonderful engine of intelligence, calling to the heart's longing for ascension, the arrow's yearning for the bow, my own struggle to my feet, propped up, the stilt walker's smile down on the faces looking up. The kite is a carnival comet banging at the end of its leash. It is the tether, the resistance, that gives it its configured life, filling with where it cannot go. I too am braced up like a kite, the trapezius muscle, the crossbow shoulders, waiting for a great wind to carry me across the sky.

In front of Provincetown library, I find my friend Vol Quitzow, one of the last street musicians left in town, playing his keyboard, his scores for movies never filmed, sonatas for dead stars whose light has just begun to reach us. I shake his hand, holding it in both of mine, this beautiful white haired old brother who brings his music to sidewalk and street as it wells up around the thighs of the walkers, circles them like mimosa smoke. Some linger to listen. Others drop change in the yellow plastic bucket. We talk about music, his decade ago arrangement of an Aaron

Copland song which he played for Copland's smiling approval. He remembers playing with Charles Mingus and gives me part of that riff on the keyboard. And poetry. Vol knew Gregory Corso from Greenwich Village days. He remembers Corso drunk in Vesuvios, San Francisco, Corso lifting his face from a puddle of vomit on the bar, still talking poetry, the blue allegory crackle of the poem never stopping, the force through which the green fuse drives the drunken flower. Vol and I meet tomorrow for coffee, noon at the Café Maria, where the kites fly. I have for him a small poem by Chiyo-ni, a Japanese woman, eighteenth century, a contemporary of Basho.

> Would that I could tie
> the string of my kite
> to the hem of your kimono.

The struggle of the kite to rise in the wind, find lodging in the sky, the longing to find a home in the heart of another, how we are bound by our natures and that of the world. It would never work: this string, that hem. The poem raises that to our knowing, a kite in the mind's sky, the cultivated heart at the end of its rope.

The next morning, when I get to Café Maria, after picking my way along crowded Commerical st., the wind has shifted to the S.E. Then straight out of the east. The kites mill around in confusion. I sit at the outside table. Maria brings out a cappuccino and a Portuguese sweet roll, kisses me on the cheek and waves away the ten dollar bill I had folded length wise. *See how you are,* I call after her as she is about to step back into the café. She turns around. *That is how I am.* Then she laughs. It is the turning around I love. The heart of the story of Orpheus and Eurydice, the hard spike of knowing, is when and why Orpheus turns back to her as they are climbing the dark stairway out of hell, back up into the world of light, trees and rivers. Of course, he turned back to find her with his eyes. I would have turned back. I do turn back every morning I awake to those behind me, their hands reaching, fingers like sea grass. When Maria looks back around, winter turns in its grave of snow, six months to the north, and dreams of a carnival forest of kites beside Café Maria.

Always here in Provincetown, I think about the whales out off the cape, Stellwagen bank, twenty miles out, a great underwater mountain thrusting to within eighty feet of the surface, hundreds of whales feeding and playing there every summer. Last year, I went out four times. One

188

evening the *Portuguese Princess* was surrounded by humpbacks, spouting, sounding, singing, a chorus of silky granite, sky creatures fallen. I meet the naturalist from the whale watching boat *The Captain Red*, Dennis Minsky, bicycling down Commercial street. He pedals over to shake my hand. *Good thing you went last summer with us to see the whales. They're not on the bank this summer. Most days, it's just a boat ride.* Dennis thinks it may be the nine and a half mile long sewer pipe Boston ran out into the Atlantic, belching the treated waste out into Cape Cod bay. The water is too rich with nitrogen. Gone are Compass and her calf. Gone are Foxfire and the old grandmother who returned from Caribbean winter grounds for twenty five summers. Someone flushes a shitter in Jamaica Plain; a humpback and her calf turn toward the open Atlantic.

Third day. I make a cup of late morning tea, take up my notebook and Czeslaw Milosz's *A Book of Luminous Things*, a collection of poetry, pages of lighted candles. I buttwalk to the kitchen door and open it into the yard. The Cape Cod sun knifes every shadow, holds it for the eye in sun washed attention. I prop open the door, arrange things as if setting up camp and lie on the rug, the book out in the sun field. I drift into Rumi's poem.

> Out beyond ideas of wrongdoing and rightdoing,
> there is a field. I'll meet you there.
>
> When the soul lies down in that grass,
> The world is too full to talk about.
> Ideas, language, even the phrase each other,
> doesn't make any sense.

Marty Epp, a local painter, crosses the yard toward me, her gazelle step, moon face smile, and sits on the door step. I give her the Rumi poem from memory. She listens with closed eyes. The poem is a dragonfly she has swallowed, its winged life in her always. She smiles, thanks me, springs away, lopes across the field, buries herself in the day to rise later in the waters of her painting. An offshore breeze springs up. In a moment the heat is gone. The painter Bert Yarborough wanders by to fetch his beach towel off the clothesline. He is headed out to Herring Cove to come clean. For him, the work is always to keep the painting open and alive, the canvas as field of contention, the old argument against the king's law and the gnome's rulebook, extending the wings in the updraft, horizon the only boundary. *We learn to paint with hope*, Bert laughs. I remind him of Emily Dickinson's lines: "Hope is that feathered thing that perches in the soul..." *We've been painting with seagull feathers out on the dunes,* Bert tells me and waves goodbye to the landlubber. Everything leads back into itself. No time to tell him about my year long poem listing my bet to win on every horse I came across with the word hope in its name, how I didn't bet a horse, how I got shut out, at Turfway park this spring on a horse named King Hope who paid $156.00 to win on a two dollar ticket. Hope is always a long shot king, blinded by every sunrise but still he plays the sky gift harp, and we listen. I don't bother Bert with the old joke about the difference between a woman in the bathtub and a woman in church: the woman in church has hope in her soul.

The fourth day. Lu comes back to the cottage at noon, from working in the July sun-beat studio, flushed and happy, dirty, heated to the heart. On the back of her right thigh runs an odd black inked calligraphy, dirty work sweat and charcoal streaked into a headless kokopelli, a wind wrecked tabernacle, a crisscrossed sky of black vapor trails. She must have rubbed up against an outcropping of the world and it rubbed back. Or a ghost writer kneewalked behind her, black lighting a runic massage. I am a student of this language. It is explicit; the shape of its meaning is clear. *Lie down with me in this meadow.* To the iron eyes, it reads *wash me, don't walk around like this.* At Herring Cove beach, Lu wades out into the Atlantic, sixty three degrees today, two-three foot waves. Then, she swims on out, dark otter head bobbing against rumpled silver. When she walks back to me, drying in the sun, and turns to look at the water, I see the script has faded. Tomorrow, after soap and shower, the skin slate will be empty. I hold it here, on the page. *Lie down with me in this meadow.*

Maria brings me another cappuccino, sweet froth, bitter pleasure. No charge. Enjoy this day. A quick smile. In a couple of days, LuAnn and I will be staying at Carlos and Maria's house, up on Tiny Way, behind the Pilgrims' monument, that two hundred and fifty seven foot granite memorial to those who put out to sea and could not find their way back. This afternoon, near my outdoor table at the bricked sidewalk's end, at beach's edge, a mermaid has crawled ashore, covered herself with sand, and now sits against a boulder, her tail extended, hair curling over one breast, flat belly, nipples hard, hostage in the upper world. I roll over to the sand sculptor and ask him, *What time did this mermaid wash ashore? Last night. And you just covered her with sand and set up the tip jar?* His name is Scott Dasch, balding, short ponytail guy, barefoot, quick of eye, perfumed with whiskey. With his eyes and patter, he keeps rein on his two small children, a three year old boy and a girl about four, who sit beneath the kite shop awning painting themselves with ice cream. Like a gypsy, he brings his children with him to town. The money in the bucket is for them. *Please support the arts. Thank you. We are not supported in any other way. Thanks for your donation for the photograph. It takes me about four hours. A different sculpture every day. Donations not required but thank you. My family and I do new stuff everyday.* I ask him her name, the mermaid's. *This is Ariel's big sister Aureole.* Aureole will live til sundown, after the whale watching crowds wander by with their Boston dollars. Then the undoing. The impermanence of form. All of this is going away in accordance with its own nature. Flesh is sand and everything full of tears. Aureole, let me go down in my dreams.

I look up and, inside the restaurant, Maria is making sandwiches. In silhouette against the open back door, she is holding a leaf of lettuce above a sandwich. She pauses as if giving me time to keep the shaded moment, looks up, smiles, then closes the lid on the sandwich. It is done. The old everything is done. A young blonde woman with a bare belly walks by the table. A man carries a crying child. The elixir of apple juice won't stop his tears. Outside Himalayan Handicrafts next door hang a dozen dresses, pleading in the breeze for shoulders, knees, arms, feet to walk them away. Maria pops out to sit with me at the sidewalk table, searches my eyes and asks, in her Portuguese English, *Are you boring yet?* No one has ever asked me that. The answer is yes. I tell her no.

At midnight, a storm blows up over the Atlantic and marches over this thin peninsula, distant thunder, then thunder in the yard, lightning in the gladiolas. Lu and I lie naked in the bed, washed in that surf, the hard rain scrubbed breeze, the curtains standing out like ghost aprons. An alarm kicks on in the Fine Arts Work Center common room next door, a stuck wail that cuts through every thought. After 15 minutes, someone finds the switch.

We sleep deep under the doom of rain washed air. I get to Café Maria about two in the slow afternoon. Vol comes bounding up the street. He hands me a priority mail envelope with five pages: first is his rendition of Michelangelo's sketch of the head of a young woman, sideview, the classical line of the long nose, mouth firmly set, as if she is looking inward at a world we cannot see. The story goes back ten years. Minutes after he had sketched her face from a book in the Provincetown library, Vol walked into the Portuguese bakery and there she stood behind the counter. Her name was Sonya Santos. Vol painted six pastels of her. He shows copies of each to me. It is Michelangelo's young

191

woman, without a doubt. She has always been with us, a dream of beauty we replenish nightly. Vol then sculpted in clay her head as she posed. He shows me a photo of that. Then another page entitled *Sculptured bust backed by a toy moon inspired by Sonia Santos, living reincarnation of a Michelangelo drawing of a young girl —wash rendering of paper.* On the paper, Sonia's beautiful, still face stares back, though never directly, always off to the side, as if she is holding at bay something nameless with her eyes, a black dog, a cold sunrise. Vol leaves her with me, all the faces on paper, her toy moon orbiting over my head. I fumble with Jung's notion of the anima, how each man carries from childhood the enfolded image of an ideal woman. Over a lifetime, it opens like a lotus. The search is for that woman in the world. Seldom does the actual meet the ideal, the pilgrim poking his head through heaven's ceiling. If it does, the outcome is always tragic. Even in his copy of the Michelangelo sketch, Vol bent some lines away from the fearful ideal. No one could reach there and live.

Saturday we awake to cold fog, our last day in the Fine Arts Work Center cottage. We pack, linger, find our way down to Maria's. The sand sculptor Scott is asleep in the beach grass, his two little children wandering and playing with the whirligig kites staked in the sand. Ada, the beautiful young woman who stays with Vol, keeps a restive eye on them. She walks toward me, *Not my kids,* she says. *Not my problem.* Ada is a restless, clear eyed spirit, Santa Cruz, New Orleans, a street performance artist, maybe late twenties, coltish, dead level gaze, lived for a year with Bill Iverson. Do I know him? Yes, his poems, under the name Brother Antoninus, his poetry an argument with himself and his god, his Franciscan vows the old war of flesh and spirit reflected in the polished shield of his poems. Ada leaves to get ready for her two thirty street performance in front of town hall. She costumes and imagines herself into Buzzette—a Raggedy Ann, spring-driven doll, lockjointed, rouge cheeked, with some kind of digitalized audible buzz device strapped on her belly she controls with a palm squeeze to accompany each movement. Or for all I know the answer is what Buzzette told an inquisitive child: she gulped down a handful of crickets and told them she would set them free at summer's end if they would, at her command, rub their legs together and chirp in unison. The child swallowed it. So did I, along with most explanations I get. Gimpel the fool taught me if it is not true here, it probably is true somewhere else, if not now, then later.

Buzzette has drawn a crowd of forty or more. She marches squeaksquawk up to a bald, back pedaling onlooker, pursues him with red-painted puckered lips. Finally he leans toward her beckoning kiss. Buzzette ducks his advance, plopping her head on his chest, to the delight and laughter of everyone. She machine strides back to her post, turns, four clicks down into a bow and applause. She stands up as Ada, announcing she is a street performance artist supported solely by donations. The bucket fills, tourist dollars. Everyone seems disarmed by the loving, harmless deception, the comic courtship, the beautiful woman mimicking a doll with a bellyful of ghost crickets. At the edge of the crowd, an old man sends a winged prayer. *Ada, you see what I am. Change me.* I ask her where Buzzette was born. *In the factory of love in Montreal.* I swallow that, too.

A Little Poem for Ada
Tell me how things are.
I believe you know.
If Vol is going away,
Where is he going?
How do you know?
What is spirit made of?
Those crickets you swallowed,
What do they sing about?
And for whom?
Tell me one thing to keep.

At the FAWC common room, Saturday night, Stanley Kunitz speaks to an overfull room about his friendship with Theodore Roethke, dead forty years. He and Kunitz were poetry pups together, adversaries over the tennis net and in the poppy field of poetry. Kunitz's profile, I'm sitting ten feet to his left, is defined by a laureate's eagle beak, a pathfinder, a starpointer, a Pontiac hood ornament, a beauty as memorable as Durante's or W.C. Field's. But this is a diamond cutter, a poet's hatchet for falling the hardwoods in truth's dark forest. He'll be ninety eight years old tomorrow, the oldest tree on the mountain. He is beautiful, this man. Winds long gone from this world have bent those branches. His roots drink the rain of other centuries. All of that is in his voice. He mouths the words as if each were a pebble. I carry away this: Kunitz quoting Henry James about his art — *My doubt is my passion.* All the good poets I know eat the doubt of their own words. O mother of doubt, abide with me, quicken the embarrassment that I speak at all upon these pages. Tie my shoelaces. Trip me. Keep me here on my skinny ass, sitting in the middle of poetry's sidewalk, one shoe off, one shoe on, penciling a poem for my tall son Sean.

The sandman pulls up a chair next to me at Café Maria. His children join us, little John William, three or so, and Dylan Marie, a beautiful, freckled four year old, a purple feather boa round her neck. Scott, the sandman, says they were sick last night in the campground where they've been living. No place they can afford in P'town, thanks to greed. His wife Jessica pulls up in a taxi. She is twenty three, long legged, a dancer in every step. Scott has been kicked off his work place where the public beach abuts the bricked walk of the kite shop. He can no longer use the three foot tall marker rock against which to lean his mermaid sculpture. Some of the wet sand always found its way onto the bricked sidewalk. The kite shop manager fussed it away with an industrial broom. The wind blew it back. Out came the broom. Finally, the owner. Then the police chief. Yesterday, the owner kicked the sand mermaid to death. Scott walked away, gathering his kids. He just moved down the block, sat up in front of a shop named the Mystic Moon, another toy moon orbiting beauty's brow. It is the duty of a free man to oppose the times in which he finds himself.

The last sculpture I watched him make, I asked him not to put the P'town beach sunglasses on the mermaid. *I want to see her eyes,* I said. *Let me look into her eyes.* I was drinking coffee at an outdoor table at Maria's, when Scott called, *Hey, Maj.* Twenty feet away she was looking right at me, Aureole, the tangerine breasted sand princess, reclined against the rock, staring at a world in which there was nothing for her to love, the gaze of a prisoner from a barred window at a sea below. The face, I saw for the first time, was that of the sandman's four year old daughter Dylan Marie, little freckled boa dancer translated on through the years, washed ashore in lunklaw land, property lines drawn, the golden calves prodded down the street. Oh, little Dylan Marie, may my prayers guard your winged, scaled life. Little water dragon, swim toward the deep open Atlantic, through that cathedral of light. Little John William, plant your sword in the sand. Loving spirits hover round you. They defend you with their fingers of wind, the longbow of breath. Scott the sandman, stay free. Opposition feeds the numbed heart. It awakens the bear who has been sleeping in the tree, paws in his mouth, the bear who went over the mountain and is trying to find his way back to us, the bear who is drunk with the borealis honey and brings home to us a dripping comb hugged under each arm. The bear is brother to the sandman. He knows that the domed citadels of law, the dormitories of folded kites, the bricked pattern of sidewalks, are all opposed to the act of shaping the free sand by a free man into this homage the wind and the sea wear away, no axes, no taxes. You are dying, whispered the sand mermaid, to the angry kite shop owner who kicked in her belly, her head. Full moon tonight, high tide washing around the feet of the P'town sphinx, salt water eddy round the dancer's knees, lobsters clacking tong hands over church pews. The gypsy sand family rides the raft of heaven's door, waving to those who would not leave what owned them, gypsy sand family guided through the shoals by a mermaid and fixed, forgiving stars.

Bill Kennedy calls to send along the news that the old lion of Cleveland, that apostle of loneliness, Daniel Thompson, the poet, sweet potato friend, is in the Cleveland Clinic, leukemia. The past few weeks, he had strength only to crawl the floor. In the clinic, the blood dipstick measured Daniel ten pints low. Of the normal thirteen pints, Daniel was down to three, sloshing around in the bottom of the oil pan. Today, I carry big, bewhiskered Daniel on my shoulders around Provincetown. Sparrows of sorrow, wrens of redemption, nest in his whiskers, sing to my brother Daniel all night.

On Commercial street, on the way to the post office, Lu and I find the sandman finishing a sand sculpture of the Buddha, a toadstool three footer squatting in front of the Mystic Moon. I tell Scott this is a Ho-Ti Buddha he's birthed, the jolly, big eared mountain Buddha who came down in the Chinese villages with a sack on his back, gifts for the children. Santa, Sante, Saint, Santos Buddha, Sonya Santos big with compassion. He would spill his gifts on the ground and talk with the children. Not to the adults. No gifts for them. Not a word for them. Then, he'd return to his hermitage where the clouds swallowed the mountain. Today he sits on the bricked sidewalk here in P'town. Scott broods over his samsara sandman with a water spray bottle, keeping him moist lest he fall apart. Scott points to the eave of the shops. *About three o'clock he'll be in shadow.* Buddha sits resolute, silently riding the windhorse of one long sustained twenty five hundred year old breath. Scott has tipped the donation pickle basket so the passersby can see the nestle of dollars and add their own token of appreciation. This is Scott's daughter's birthday, little Dylan Marie. She has turned five. But he is working, missing her birthday. In Welsh, Dylan means *keeper of the wave*, a sandman's ally. I roll back to the Himalayan shop and buy her a bright yellow silk shoulder bag emblazoned with the Tashi Taget, the Tibetan symbol of good luck. *Auspicious*, says Chomo, the owner. Lu walks it down to Scott, standing guard over he who stands guard, who arms each of us with the sharp sword with which to hack the knot of insatiable longing. As I write this, I caress that knot, admire the intricacy of its design, how it has blunted every blade.   Good luck, little Dylan Marie, Buddha child, daughter of sand.

Everyday I make a small pilgrimage to Chomo Lama's shop, Himalayan Handicrafts.   I buy my daughter Megan a beautiful sunflower Tibetan wraparound dress, a string of prayer flags for my porch and Green Tara incense for the poet Ray McNiece who told me a year ago he prayed for her mercy.   Have a Green Tara toke on me, broken hearted golden minstrel.   Chomo, early forties, small charm-struck Tibetan face, is happy today, a royal purple shawl around her small shoulders. *How is your day, Chomo?*   I love to say her name to her.   Chomo.   In Tibetan, she is Tsering Tsomo which means *long life ocean*.   For Americans browsing her shop, she has become Chomo Lama.   Chomo.   Sounds like a machete bringing down sugar cane, the little chug of the uphill heart, Chomosome, Chomo.   Chomo smiles. *I'm doing nonsense work*, she says.   She goes to the shop's corner dressing room to retrieve and rehang a couple of dresses a woman tried on and didn't like. *Nonsense work, just around and around.   Like a moon*, I tell her.   The showcase is bedecked with India and Tibetan jewelry.   I just bought a turquoise silver ring here last week.   I want more.   I try on a hammered silver bracelet studded with coral and lapis lazuli, hold it up to the light.   Chomo fixes her dark eyes on my nonsense. *You have too much jewelry already.   Mindful should be your jewel.* I take off the bracelet.   Why do I want it?   Will it make me more beautiful or bring to me those who hide from me?   I hand it back to Chomo, make gasho.   I remind myself of my daily prayers and say them back to her, the three determinations.

> Let the mind rest on the dharma.
> The dharma rest on poverty.
> Poverty rest on death.

Let me be so determined.   Let me not become attached to things.   Let me regard passing beauty as dew on the eyelids.   Chomo tells me her friend wants to be reincarnated as a bird. *I want to fly*, I say. *In another life? No, right now, through the streets, touching the walkers with my finger tips lightly on their shoulders as I glide among them.*   Chomo looks hard at me. *Next lifetime*, she laughs, little silver bells in her throat.

Two more days in Provincetown.   It's Sunday.   Ten o'clock coffee on the Silva's back porch. *Time to get up, no more sleep*, sings out Maria.   I can begin to feel the leaving in my chest, the thickening, the unease in my sternum. The four of us drive out to the dunes, past Race Point on the Atlantic side. As residents, the Silvas have a permit to drive the dune roads. First, we deflate the tires on the four wheel drive to twelve pounds, then wallow through the sand rutted back roads, finally cresting a high dune to face the open Atlantic spread out before us. It's a two seater Toyota truck, Carlos and I in the front, Maria and LuAnn blanket wrapped in the open bed. We talk back and forth through the sliding back window. Carlos pulls up the little truck at the ocean's edge and turns off the engine. *Across there is Portugal, a long way.* He and Maria came here in their teens. The four of us sit quiet for a while. A lobster boat runs full throttle a half mile out, parallel to the shore. He cuts the boat engine, drifts. Carlos says, *He's checking his nets. Each boat is allowed ten traps, hard work. You have to weight them with rocks to keep them on bottom.* Everything is close yet far, four bodies in the steel body of the truck, the big wash of the open Atlantic, the lobster traps resting, baited.

Lu and I excuse ourselves just after dinner on the back porch with the Silvas, more scallops, chicken, sirloin, potatoes. The poet Alan Dugan reads tonight at the FAWC common room across town. He is eighty four now, walks haltingly, a brace on his left leg. Mine is on the right. Last year, he won the National Book award for his collection of poetry *Seven Poems*. He included every poem he'd ever published, no cuts, the complete record. Tonight, he reads maybe ten poems. The early ones are New York salty, leftist, man caught in the machinery, bleak. Then, he reads a poem about two butterflies mating, winged humping, how the fruit of the conception is a worm, how we are asked to trust the transformation to come. As the butterflies disengage, they rise in a north wind in the long ride to Mexican uplands. Swallows hunt them so skillfully, they snatch only the bodies, leaving the severed lifeless wings to drift down to earth. If the butterflies make it to the trees of Mexico, they must die *in a crowd, in a crowd*, each by each in a crowd, the loneliness of death among the many. It was a line that rattled my bones. Just before Dugan read that poem, someone in the back of the room was stricken with what I don't know. But, it was a loud *ouf*, an exhaled groan, a cry for something. There was a hum of concern, a circle around someone down on the floor. A man was carried from the muggy common room. EMS arrived. He was carted away, a butterfly sideswiped by a Sunday night swallow no one else could see, a wing span touching the door frame as it glided through, searching for him in the crowd. Ah, Dugan, old hammered heart, solitary. Whatever good we do in this world, this impulse begins when we are alone. For the evil, we find collaborators and apologists on every hand. Dugan, a man more salt than sugar, is a handful of sand in poetry's washing machine. Finally, he reads a beautiful, tender elegy about a mouse caught in a trap. I thought of W.C.W.s *Sparrow: to My Father*, the final image of that small bird flattened on a city street by a truck tire, emblem of things gone, his last words, the bird's, the man's. *Farewell. I have done my best.* I pound my hands together for Dugan, who himself applauds with his bony hands, salutes, forgives, wishes us farewell.

Last morning in Provincetown. I say goodbye to Chomo at her shop, already busy with tourists ferried over from Boston and Plymouth. In the midst of the bustle, she asks, *You want tea?* Yes. She brings out hot Tibetan tea, thick with milk and sugar, in plastic cups, one couched inside the other. *I have come for a last lesson*, I tell her. *No last lesson*, Chomo laughs. Then she writes this question on the back of a business card. A couple of seminarian students had been browsing in the shop. The talk led to their theology studies. One of them had written this question on a scrap of paper and handed it to Chomo who passes it to me. *What am I doing that I can't see?* What does it mean, asks Chomo. The answer comes like a sparrow through the open door of the shop. I remember Rumi's lines: *One should spend as much time doing the invisible work as one does at the visible.* What you can't see is that invisible work. *What is it*, Chomo frowns, *this invisible work?* I tell her: feeding the soul, prayer, meditation, befriending yourself behind the ribs' jail, painting holy images on the walls of the inward house, paying devout attention, sitting empty with every hungry ghost from the four corners, painting the soul's windows with breath, tears and pollen, riding the white horse across a snowstorm in the chest, the invisible scaffolding that the trusting foot finds and begins its ascent toward the sky hole, the soft spot in the skull. It seemed clear enough then. Later, I remembered Blas de Otero's words. *God protect me from seeing what is clear.* The lines from Chomo's shop tilt. They become admonition. *What is it I am doing that keeps me from seeing?* I smell like a man who believes he has answered the question: burnt hair, sour clothes, the sweetness of rust. Chomo, I don't know. I am as blind as a Louisville slugger. Take me by the shoulders and turn me toward the door. I am going home.

The last day of July, Lu and I drive out of Provincetown, down route 6, fourteen hours from Kent. Ten miles south at Wellfleet, the last of the beached Pilot whales are dying, forty six in all, ninety degree lowtide sun baking them dead. Several hundred people have gathered, a bucket brigade, wet blankets. Lu and I don't go to see them. It is too ferocious in its sadness, too wounding. Idle witness has always seemed wrong to me. I can't fix this. Yesterday, fifty six of them piled up on a beach near Dennis, twenty miles south of Provincetown. Rescuers shepherded forty six of them back to sea on the high tide, walking them to deep water. The pod swam up to Wellfleet and followed the leader onto another beach. Rescuers again waded them out on the midday tide, trained wildlife personnel and vacationers, on back out to the open sea to the applause of hundreds of bystanders. Then hours later, the whales charged the Wellfleet beach again, wallowing as far as they could, sometimes stacking atop one another, clumping on the salt marsh. This time the whales were so exhausted, their heartbeat so weak, they began to die in the crush of their weight stranded on land. Veterinarians walked among them, euthanizing them each by each. Onlookers reported the whales talked among themselves in their language of click and whistle, a sound like sneakers on a gym floor, the air cryptic with the breathed jot of farewell and loss. The dead whales were scooped up by backhoes and hauled away in army trucks. The plan was to rope together the bodies, tow them far out to sea, weight them with concrete and sink the pod, now reunited in the deep from which it came.

It may by as simple as follow the leader. Pilot whales live in the familial linkage of a pod, an extended family of up to two hundred. The Pilots are members of the dolphin family, much more social than other whales, easily trained. The pod follows a respected leader. The sand bars around Cape Cod shift, realign themselves, after every storm. The graveyard of ships and sailors, it is also that for the Pilot whale. The cape was glacially formed only fifteen thousand years ago. Our navigational records date back only four hundred years. Perhaps there were once channels across the cape that have since filled with sand, and the Pilot whale carries a genetically imprinted map of what is no longer there. Does not each of us turn toward what beckons at the edge of gone. A leather glove nailed to an oak in the deep woods; a young woman in a yellow dress, wading a mountain stream, a wand of willow; the shadowy scaffolding of a farmhouse on a windswept hillside, the front door ajar; a cemetery sleeping beneath the asphalt of a parking lot, the dead counting our footsteps; shoes without feet, the years without words. You go ahead. I'll follow. I trust you with my life.

UP THE STAIRS I RISE TO WAKE THE MOON: EULOGY, DANIEL THOMPSON'S FUNERAL, CHURCH OF THE COVENANT, CLEVELAND, OHIO, MAY 10, 2004

Daniel was, for years, a puckish and welcome intruder in our house in Kent, a first story man. My wife LuAnn would sometimes look up from her reading or work at hand and say, *I think Daniel is coming to visit.* He would barge through the door unannounced, unbidden, like one of D.H. Lawrence's strange angels. *Admit them, admit them*, urges Lawrence in his poem. Admit him, we did, gladly. I never got past the bright map of his face, though I do recall he always stomped into the house, a bow legged twostep. His face, an impish grin as if he had let the air out of one of my tires or picked all of the preacher's tulips or committed a misdemeanor for love or justice or both. He arrived hungry. He couldn't eat everything because of his diabetes, but he ate all of everything else, with lip smacking, polishing the plate with bread gusto. Then, the stories would start. Half the people Lu and I didn't know in his Damon Runyon /Mickey Spillane/ Dostoevski/ Cleveland intrigue epics. We listened, not for the facts or the cavalcade of pilgrims in progress, but for whatever it was that moved Daniel, made him rise up in delight, whatever was behind those words like a bee swarm round his head.

In the poetry of Virgil, we find the phrase *lacrimae rerum*, the tears of things, an old and abiding pity, what brokenness knows deep in the chest. Daniel always understood that there are tears inside everything, even words. Especially words. Daniel knew that words are also full of honey. Honey and tears are the marrow of words. Daniel, the poet of tears. Daniel, the poet of honey. Daniel, the poet of vinegar and salt. Daniel, big whiskered wooly hummingbird, found ways everyday to drink from the moment's source, the orange trumpet vine, the blue morning glory, the sweet pea blossom, the rose with petals of concrete, the rusted sunflower.

The first night after Daniel stepped into the shadows, Lu and I lit candles, in mason jars, and set them out on the front steps. I couldn't shake the thought of Daniel flying overhead, circling the earth, unfettered, tumbling like an otter, paddling along on his back, cracking oyster shells with a rock, eating the poems he found inside, pitching the shells down to earth — check your backyard — playing in the Aurora Borealis surf, doing loop de loops through the magnetic static of the Van Allen belt, a swimmer in the waning moonlight. Sustained, safe, in the long orbit which cradled him. These candles are navigation lights, little lamps of grief, votive flames of gratitude, little bonfires of love and friendship, landing lights on the deck of the mothership, Krishna's chicory eyes, a constellation in the sky beneath our feet, little tongues of fire making words in the darkness. Light a candle tonight before you sleep your own little death. Set it out under the open sky for the freedom train flyer. Guide him home. All things are an exchange of fire: fire to fire; naked heart to naked heart.

The body is a temporary home. There are only things continually arising and passing away, as is their nature. Everything is preparing to disappear. If you understand this your heart will ease. Love hard. Pay attention. Be grateful.

As Daniel lay in the hospital bed, Cleveland Clinic, Wednesday afternoon, May 5, Cinco de Mayo, the day before he left, I held his hand and watched his labored breathing beneath the oxygen mask for a couple of hours, the rise and fall of his chest. The abode of his loving heart. Where is breath before we breathe it? If we understand that, we are home. Daniel is going home. In his poems, he mapped the way, blue highways, asphalt, gravel, dirt lowways, a footpath. From there on, it is unmarked. We walk shoeless in the dark. Our homesickness is our guide. Trust that. If you were homeless, you'd be home right now, right here.

Daniel has gone away. No one knows where away is. It may not be far. Away may be no more than the space between two breaths, two heartbeats, or two words, like food, love, home, sing.

Farewell to the poet who kept the watch with the saints in the city and weathered the midnight air.

Farewell to the poet who played the flute cut from articulate bone, music that flowed like a stream of light.

Farewell to the poetry fool who did persist in his folly till he became wise. Few have gone as far down that unmarked trail as Daniel did, hauling the dark cargo of the heart.

Farewell to the poet who wrote his valentine in the ghost snow, who knew that anguish is still the world's official language.

Farewell to the beekeeper stung by death, to the poet who made honey of old failures and regrets. Each poem is a jar of that honey. Each taste carries a blessing, even if hidden. O taste and see.

Farewell to the poet whose question has gone unanswered: *O America, cold machine in high fever/Why must you devour the young?*

Farewell to the poet who sang to the lone sparrow caught in the thicket.

Farewell to the poet who knew we all share one loneliness and one need to break bread and out of that broken silence tumbles everything.

Farewell to the poet who was singular in his disturbance, whose dreams cut like a knife.

Farewell to the poet who was one with the dumb and stood up for the stupid and the crazy.

Farewell to the poet whose cock and bully days are done yet his heart, still shining, sings.

Farewell to the poet who left a trail of breadcrumb words for the alphabet birds that follow us all.

Farewell to the poet who knew we all save coupons no one will redeem except in darkness. Sorrow. Sorrow. Sorrow.

Farewell to the poet who drank the bitter dregs of Winesburg in the dark laughter of rain.

Farewell to the nocturnal poet who stepped through the crack, before dawn, Thursday morning, May 6, not into the heartless dark but into that cornucopia of light for which he yearned.

Farewell to the poet who waited sixty nine years for the weather to break. This day the weather has broken like a river in our hearts.

> O listen to the silence and the words
> And the silence and the words and the silence
> And the words and the silence....and the words
> And the silence.

Farewell to the poet who this day comes to ground zero, upon the down of earth to rest. Safe passage to Daniel whose name we call out into the honeyed air of eternity. Daniel. Now, quiet as a star.

CHRISTMAS FALLS ON ST. BERNARD'S CHURCH
—Akron, Ohio

My daughter Megan and I set out
to Christmas shop, Summit mall,
big glass American marketplace, wide eyed scramble,
paper money for things, tokens of our longing
to be received with gratitude, thanksgiving gobbled and gone.

At two dollars an hour, plus tips,
Meg has saved one hundred and forty dollars
in her zip up purse. It won't be enough.
Last night, I parked out front
of the Kentwood restaurant where she is a server.
Let her serve, not wait.
I sat in the car for half an hour,
the tall cold windows between us,
and watched Meg carry trays of food,
fill coffee cups, moving gracious and smiling
among the old couples, the golden buckeye lovers.
She never saw me.
I steered out into the concrete darkness
of route 59, the bug eyed busyness of traffic.
Stay in your own lane.

Meg says it's all work and school,
no time for poems or drinking rain,
picking ripe peaches on the tundra.
What if it's charred hearts, GPA,
taxes and pancake makeup from here on out.
We cross the Y bridge into Akron.
The twin spires of St. Bernard's church
rear against the sooted skyline,
the frozen music of praise
aimed toward the low gray ceiling of this heaven.
Everything around the church has collapsed,
the old bus terminal bulldozed, stores boarded.
Only the cop shop thrives,
the police cruisers lined up like army tanks
along the curbs of this Goodyear carcass town.
We find a side door, a ramp, and roll step
into the vaulted, chilled quiet.

The statues, the pews, the stained glass windows,
the votive flames, all seem to stop moving
inside themselves just as we open the door.
Meg and I sit near the front of the empty church,
long minutes, the ticking of stone.
We bow, unguarded.
Behind us the voices of children,
small laughter, clamber among the pews.
Their father wanders the stations of the cross,
hands in pockets, as if window shopping for a gift.
They fade into silence. A door closes.

Somewhere below us, steps, muffled voices.
Quiet. The sorrowful mother, to our left,
stares down in stony repose at the two of us.
Meg and I link hands, in thanks for what
has brought us here, for what has joined our hearts.
I hear my voice, worn but clear.
An old bud of bone, something in me,
has never bloomed, a fist of petals.
It is from this I pray.
A gray priest appears from the side
of the altar, a stooped shuffle.
He welcomes us, asking our names. *Ragain.*
Is that Irish? Yes. Ah, he says,
*only two kinds of people. Those who
are Irish and those who want to be.*
Me, he announces, *I'm a Kraut,
my parents from Alsace Lorraine.
They were married in this church.
My name is Father Reymann.
You may stay as long as you like.*

He turns. I won't let him go.
Father, will you bless us?
He lays his old hands on our foreheads,
makes his slash mark in the name
of the other father whose face
is the midnight sun, in the name
of his son who set free the meek sparrow.
He invokes the holy spirit
whose name no man knows.

When I open my eyes, he is gone.

Akros, the high place.
Tinsel on the hanging tree.
Gather round us,
little sisters of raw,
little brothers of ruin,
cold mother, bent father.
Share with us this supper,
flat bread, black honey and salt,
in God's house of marble tears.

Letter to My Grandfather Roy Everett Ragains From his Grandma Watkins, Mailed from Caldwell, Idaho, to Paris Illinois, February, 21, 1909

my dear boy i will anseer your letter so glad to here fromyou and here you was well grandpa and i are well of course your ant nettie ant very well she hasent walked a step for allmost a year i am afraid she never will walk again roy rite to her it will do her good anut bessie lives in caldwell rite to her dident you git the baby card with er picture on it she sent you one and alviah too tell me when ther you got them or not it was aunt bessie baby picture well you got lots for christmas i got a nice plate that all i got well what is you mama doining this winter i guess she is to busy to rite me i rote the last letter and i have lots to do i have 4 boarders and it keeps me busy i git four dolars a week that makes me 10 dollars well roy the 21 of april i will be 60 years old and granpa will be 61 we are getting old and you soon will be a young man you and alviah and edgar you sad you had a gun be curfil with it roy there is so many killed wiht guns your granpa dont hunt anymore he cant see very good well roy allways be a good boy and rite to me and i will allways rite to you and alviah as long as i live and never forget your dear old gramma for she thinks lots of you and alviah i want to rite some to alvia and your gramma so tell your mama to rite well roy i have got 3 white cats thare pretty as white as snow and i have got about 90 white lagern chicken they are pretty and good to lay it hasent bin very cold here hasent bin down to zero 6 above is as cold as it ever gits we havent had much snow it snow a little and then the sun comes out and dryes it out it dont staye vary ;long your aunt nettie lives 6 miles west of us they have 80 acres of land and are giting along all rite making lots of mony rite to edgar and ethel there adress is greenlief idaho tell your mama to rite to your aunt nettie it would do her good well roy it is diner time and i must quit for this time rite soon and often from you dear old granma and pa

so good by you dear boy

Hair of the Head/A Visitation, 1997

The Hale Bopp comet, how far it has come. I saw it for the first time last night, low in the northwest, a smear of light caught in the bare branches. The ice core is a dust ball, twenty five miles in diameter. It is burning, though not in a way I can understand. A fiery snowball held in a glowing coma, an envelope of frozen smoke a million miles across. Tonight, the comet rides just below the starry chair of Cassiopeia and the constellation of Perseus who took Medusa's head. On April fools day, it will be closest to us, a kiss away, one hundred and twenty two million miles. It will swing around the sun and leave us here, frost in our eyebrows. It has come to show us how its heart burns. Look hard.

It began as a dim, fork tailed smudge of celestial light, a smear of luminescence, a tear in the black tent. It got as close as Jupiter's orbit undetected before two sleepless men saw it the same night. It is slated to return in three thousand years or so. Measure your reincarnations accordingly. Comets are fickle in their orbiting. There is no assurance of return. Ellipses can flatline. In eternity there is no posterity. Look up for the two prongs, the long tail of atomic static dragging straight behind, a short curving tail of dust. It has come to teach us an abiding radiance, a tenderness for high, cold places, that which longs to be known, its shimmering penumbra of light across our brows.

Looking off the second floor porch, St. Petersburg, Florida, little Meg and I find the comet, held in the soft evening air, riding the deepening blue, above a pale band of lingering light. It has begun its return to the deep reaches, the dark lockers, one hundred and twenty four million miles and fading. The word comet means, literally, the hair of the head. It is skull full of burning snow. A jack o lantern who swallowed a star. By eight o'clock, it has dropped below the tree line. Meg asks, *how fast is it traveling?* Given the distance it must cover, it doesn't matter.

THE CHILD IS A THUNDER-DREAMER

Little Brad Billingsley,
four year old morning patrol,
pedals up on his peewee bike,
skids to a stop,
throwing gravel on the front porch.
It is red, decaled with stars and planets,
Saturn whirling inside its rings.
Its name is *Time Raider* in gold block letters
and along the center bar the phrase *Flexible Flyer*.
This knee high, knobby tired,
handlebar antlered vehicle is tilted against
every law that holds the world together.
Little Brad, give up on pillaging
the coffers of time, the golden hours.
Give time to time, teach the Jewish fathers.
Better aspire to be a Flexible Flyer,
bending with the vagrant wind,
riding the updrafts.

THE MELON FIELDS BURN IN JULY

Driving north on U.S. 41,
out of Vincennes, Indiana,
my daughter Meg and I come upon
the late July melon fields,
acres of cantaloupes, muskmelons, honeydews.
They grow along the Wabash delta,
sandy soil fed by the river.
How do they grow? asks Meg.
The farmers plant them in hills.
They vine like green snakes.
Big yellow blossoms pump up into hard nipples.
The heat swells them into melons.
At night they toss around sleepless,
live jumping beans, tugging at the vines.
Then one morning the thumpers come
in their pickups and wagons
and roll them aboard, bump and boom.
Melons are piled roof high
along the road side.
Posey county Indiana broods on
its own meaty heart.

South of Sullivan,
we turn off at a melon stand
tended by a young woman
and three small children,
dirt legged pop sluggers.
Off to the side,
an impatient man is teaching
the ten year old burr head boy
to drive the family truck,
forward and back, let out the clutch.
A trip of ten feet. Stall. Back up.
Do it again.
Finally he leaves it
where he started,
the front bumper against the produce stand.
He still doesn't know how to drive.
The father nods to him in assent.
Whatever got done here

I don't understand.

Perhaps those gypsies fade
with the dying sunlight
and drift the fields as lunar moths,
brushing one another lovingly
with their huge velvet wings.
The truck is the ark the boy
will steer through the mountainous seas
after heaven's dam breaks at dawn.
Perhaps I have been blind from birth,
reading the magic screen on my eyelids.
The melon is the cannon ball of sunlight
that breaks the ribs of the ghost ship
in whose hold I am shackled.

We buy two melons,
a day away from ripe,
striped with green.
The mother of the fields
thumps their noggins.
Whatever is ready inside
thumps back.
She carries them to the car,
one under each arm,
the severed head of a horny saint.

THE PRONGS OF THE JACK'S FORK RIVER

My son Sean and I find our way back to the Jacks' Fork river, the Ozarks, southern Missouri. The hill country sits on a crystal clear aquifer, a single tear drop capped by limestone. Round Spring, Blue Spring, Alley Spring, Welch, Montauk, Rymer. We have been coming here from Illinois since Sean was a boy. In two days, he will be twenty seven. Windy Smith, who runs the livery at Eminence, portages us upstream forty miles to the headwaters — locals call it the Prongs. Windy leaves us at the route 17 Y bridge and, as he turns the truck toward home, asks, *Anything you boys need?* We'll be four days on the river. We wave him on. We need everything. Sean wades the old yellow Oachitaw canoe to knee deep midstream and jumps in. We are loose on the water, the current slowly turning us down river toward the riffles. It is that moment of turning I feel in my shoulders. From here, we can float to the polar ice caps. The route is open. But the light is going. We paddle a hundred yards back toward the Prongs and find a gravel bar, set up camp. Sean fires up a Coleman white gas lantern. We fish the last light, drifting down toward a group of rocks. I flip a silver Rapala in close and let the current carry it up against one of the rocks and along the backwash. The smallmouth bass hits me in the biceps, the jar of the strike. He is too big to head. I see the flash of his side as he bulldogs his way back to the sanctuary of the rock. And gone. *You had him, Pop.* Later, from our sleeping bags, we look long at the planets in the western sky, Jupiter, Mars, Venus, three evening stars, strung out in a row, once in a hundred years, the beads of a broken rosary, a three eyed water dragon clambering out of a black hole. We pass back and forth a birthday half pint of Jim Beam, its sour mash bite. A single whippoorwill sings till near dawn.

A hot, windless day on the Jack's Fork. We dip our hats in the cold river and wear them. Up above Blue Spring, there is not a single house, no roads. We drift and fish crawdads in the deep shady cuts. Sean hooks a pound and a half smallmouth, here they call them bronzebacks, near a tree stump hole. Every spring, the floods in this deep valley move the furniture around on the river, uprooting trees, building snag piles, rerouting gravel bars. You have to learn the river all over again. We ride a narrow shoot down into a blue pool several hundred feet across, ringed with sandstone cliffs. The water here seems bottomless, an aching, thunderous blue. Under the canoe drift alligator gar, two paddles long, Captain Nemo's prehistoric, armored submarine, awful in their silence. We paddle hard. We are free in its movement again. Mid afternoon. The heat bears down. *Anything you boys need?* We forgot to bring drinking water. We cup our hands and drink the Jack's Fork. We put in at a gravel bar to eat canned fruit and peanut butter sandwiches. Sean swims in the quick mindless water.

Near evening, we begin to look for a place to camp, high ground; upstream rains can swell the river in minutes. We round a bend of quick water and, a couple of hundred feet ahead, see a young couple who had passed us earlier in their canoe while we had put in to shore, the only people on the river in two days. As we get closer, we see the woman, brown haired, maybe thirty, big thighed, naked on a rock shelf, on her back, her knees bent and open. The man is dressed, sitting between her knees, kissing her breasts, moving from one aureole to the other. Sean and I and the Quachitaw are caught in the narrow chute of current, headed right for them, fifty feet away. They still don't see us. Our paddles are across the thwarts. We glide silently. The man is kissing her thighs, her fingers in his black hair. He goes deeper. She looks up. We are caught in the frame, breathing neither in nor out. She pushes him away and gropes for her scattered clothes. We are in the chute, maybe ten feet away. She swings her legs sidesaddle over the edge and slips into the water without a splash, an otter sliding off a rock, one of the most elegant motions I have ever seen. She turns to us and smiles. I could have touched her with the paddle blade. The man draws his knees up against his chest and grins a daffy dong where-did-you-come-from admission. She bobs in the water and quietly laughs, *We thought we were the only ones on the river.* At that moment, we are all together, the only ones anywhere. The Jack's Fork pulls us apart and shoots us through into the cool shade of the river willows. The lovers are behind us.

Sean and I don't say much about it. The phrase *yodeling in the canyon* gets in my head and won't go away. I wonder what he calls that act of love, but I don't ask. We camp a mile down river from the Ozark ledge lovers. We drink the rest of the birthday whiskey and talk late, tracking the evening stars down into the trees. We talk summers to come, other headwaters, the Eleven Point, the Elk. I point out the constellation, right up over the tent, high in the east, called the southern crown, its shape a tiara, a starry horseshoe or a jeweled, cupped breast.

By This Alone Are Men Made Free

At the small village of Chaironia, Greece,
on the fertile Boetian plain,
squats a great stone lion,
taller than five men.
This is the battlefield
where Phillip II of Macedon
and his son Alexander, later the Great,
crushed the combined armies
of Athens and Thebes, 338 B.C.
It was Alexander's first command.
He was eighteen.
The lion guards the common grave,
the cenotaph of the two hundred men
who fell before the Macedonian phalanxes.
Among the dead lie the men
of the Theban Sacred Band, lovers sworn,
pair by pair, to fight to each other's death.
Centuries later the tyrant Odysseseus Androutsos,
believing it to be a treasure hoard,
ordered the lion hacked to pieces.
He found nothing.
The townspeople fitted the parts
and stood the lion back on his marble plinth.
The lion is not fearsome.
His head is too small for his body,
his legs too thick, his snarl too thin.
Today, my daughter caught him
with her small orange camera.
He didn't protest.
He didn't move to stop her.

Behind the village, in the foothills that run
toward Parnassos, is an ancient amphitheater,
its tiered seats cut in stone.
I stood there and shouted a poem
that had broken out of me,
in as big a voice as I could bring.
A poem for everyone who yearns to fly
outside their own skin.
I want anyone who can hear me

to know I am not on the side
of the shiteaters.
I will not be here again.
The men, the women, the children
who have lived here
have not abandoned us.

As I drive away,
an old woman in black
steps out of the olive grove,
dragging a bundle of firewood
toward her house.
Three children, in their skullcaps
of black hair, move to the side
of the road as I pass.
The boy raises a staff
of bamboo over his head.
He wants me to see it.
If it is a weapon,
it won't be enough against the Sarissa,
the fifteen foot long spear of the Macedonians.

Who does he think he is?
I know who he is.
I offer him the gray stone of my heart.

AN ANGEL PRESIDED OVER THE BIRTH

A big wind bellied full of rain
swept over the south side of Vernor lake.
The teapot shaped wall clock was stopped at 6:38 pm
by a blue bolt that stood upright for heartbeats.
A man in a yellow rainslicker is wandering
the neighborhood with an orange flashlight,
cursing the angel of electricity who has abandoned us.
Jake the snake, the next door kid, stands in the road,
in his purple poncho, lighting kitchen matches,
holding them at arm's length till they sputter out.
My mother worries the harvest in the freezer
will go bad. I tell her nothing can go bad
because goodness is an inherent quality
and there is no place for it to go
and we shouldn't have bought the side of beef
in the first place because the first place
is the very ground of our being and shouldn't
be marked by blood. She makes a stone face at me.

My daughter Meg complains there is nothing to do
when the electricity is off so I tell her a story
about Spud Alligator and his friend Speedy
Lagoon, the sweet alligator from the moon.
Because the lights are out in their gator lodge,
they decide to hike into the Black Forest
with backpacks stuffed with snickers and ding dongs.
They become the prey of awful, bristled pig people,
hunted and driven to the cliff's edge
when a great eagle with the face
of a beautiful woman bursts out of the clouds,
lifts them in her talons, soaring above danger,
and deposits them safe in their own house
whose windows now glow with golden lights.
Meg is asleep before the eagle woman
can release her.

The neighbor with the black beard
has built a bonfire in his yard,
a stuffed chair sloshed with gasoline.
His children squeal. His dogs bark.

For a moment, it is morning.
The Central Illinois Power truck creeps down
the gravel road, poking the night with a spotlight,
looking for a blown transformer, up in the trees,
looking for a severed, eyeless head on a pole.

Last night, when I turned off interstate 70,
down onto the warm asphalt ribbon,
the last forty miles home, driving between
tall regiments of corn, fragrant as a crotch,
the moths began to flutter up into the headlights.
They rose from the tarmac by the hundreds,
a milky way of soft bodies knuckling at me,
spiraling and smacking the windshield,
a brushed smear, or they were carried
up over the car and free.
I could hardly see the road
through the August snowstorm.
We are all going home.

I want to be drunk again
with my sweet Mary, back
in the empty Teutopolis catholic church,
that first day of June,
under the stained glass garden of Gethsemane,
marking one another between the eyes
with cool holy water and sour mash love.
When I stumbled with her through the door
of Agnes Braun's tavern,
I'd lost my left shoe walking
in the muddy spring fields.
When I got through the door,
across the street from God's big house,
old maid mother of grace Agnes
came out from behind the bar
and put her arms round me.
I've been waiting for you, she said.
She called me strong Michael the angel
and whispered I'd never have to die.

IN THE MIDST OF THE ASSEMBLY HE OPENED HIS MOUTH
—after the attacks of September 11, 2001

My wife and children, I wanted to gather them to me.
I found my Sean at the other end of America,
driving to work, route 5, just south of Portland, Oregon.
Go home to your family, I told him.
My wife LuAnn called from Cleveland,
Her school on lockdown alert.
My daughter Megan greeted me with *who did it?*
I know only a name.
Maybe Osama bin Laden.
Osama bin Laden.
I have been saying the words
in my head this week.
Osama bin Laden.
A greeting. A benediction. A farewell.
Osama bin Laden.
His thin, bearded face,
his hands, talk
a language we cannot understand.
Osama bin Laden.
In the marrow of that name
is music as old as stones and blood,
the sound of a flute
cut from the leg bone of a child.

We go down to the river,
Megan and I following the bricked trail
under the main street bridge to the Kent dam,
down to the open vein of the Cuyahoga
moving slow green, murky with late summer.
Down the path wanders our neighbor,
his three little girls underfoot,
crocus chatter, safe in his step.
He spits the words: *firebomb Afghanistan*
and rake the coals.
The girls dig little hands
into a bag of chips,
wondereyed at his angry voice
beneath the bridge.

Wherever death and hate couple,
the child is terror,
his lullaby the bone flute,
in the trees,
outside my window.

Back home, Megan and I fill the birdfeeders,
niger black thistle, cracked corn, sunflower seeds.
We fill them because they are empty.
Nothing more than that.
Within minutes, a whir of chickadees, finches,
flickers and sparrows assembles at God's long table,
the vesper meal, achitter with their day's small gossip.
They are not afraid.

On the back porch squats a potted plant,
a wandering jew, grown from a broken shoot
I found outside San Damiano,
the small chapel in Assisi which Saint Francis
restored with his own hands
eight hundred years ago.
It has blushed to a deep purple,
a tiny pink blossom at the end of each stem.
A spider has worked a web securing
the wandering jew to the wooden beam.
Thousands of trips back and forth,
hoping to catch what the day brings
in that shining net of patience.

Sunday evening, the Vineyard storefront church,
Pastor Todd quotes psalm fifty seven:
Have mercy on me, O God, have mercy.
I look to you for protection.
I will hide in the shadow of your wings
until this violent storm is past.
After the service, I step out
into the soft summer evening.
The dome of heaven is clear, empty sky.

Medieval alchemists,
those apothecaries of matter and spirit,
divined that the light we see

218

is but the shadow of God's greater light.
If I can believe this,
then, from dawn to dusk,
midnight to noon,
I am held in the shadow
of those great wings,
spread above me.

Hide us, in that light.

—September 17, 2001

NOTE TO MY FRIEND THE REVEREND RUFUS LUSK

This morning, I read your sermon
delivered Sunday, September 16,
at the Prince of Peace Lutheran Church in Gaithersburg.
The waters do roar and foam,
the mountains tremble.
The peaceful life is a dream
from which we have awakened.
I think of you as the devout pilot,
your congregation the passengers in their pews.
Faith is the pole star.
The Prince marks the true north.
I am no pilot; neither am I winged.
I am earthbound with words.

All love is crazy in its presumption,
top to bottom, *agape, caritas, eros,*
that we must give ourselves
unto the keeping of the other.
There is no other way.
What is not love is fear.
Mercy and patience are the same face,
mercy looking outward, patience inward.

The rabbis, while believing He
is the judge of the universe,
delighted in calling Him *Rachmana*
— the merciful — and taught
that the world is judged by grace.

The poet Hafiz: *Even after all this time*
the sun never says to the earth,
you owe me. Look what happens
with a love like that. It lights up
the whole sky.

The judgment is to love, like that.

LIVING WITHOUT COMPLAINT
—for Ted Lyons

The words of your grandmother,
Anna Marie Kirk, you gave them to me,
Be good. Be true. Be never sad.
When my daughter Meg was four,
she would march up to you and announce,
Be sad. Be good. Be never true. Or
Be true. Be never good. Be sad.
It is hard to get it right.

Tonight, in Thessaloniki, years later,
I can't get her to sleep.
She tells me stories I want to believe,
how the goat picked up the eagle and flew away,
how the mouse tied the lion
to the lemon tree and turned him
into a Macedonian prince named Alexander.
Finally, she whispers in the darkness,
Be warm. Be sleepy. Be never lonesome.

Somewhere, it is morning.
An old man steps out
into the cold shadow of a narrow street.
He does not look up.
He has not been hungry for years.
He and his basket are going to market.

What Might Save Us

It is white out across northeast Ohio,
pillars of snow driven against the house.
My daughter Meg and I make soup
in the warm kitchen,
black beans, yellow rice,
onions, garlic and red peppers
sautéed in olive oil.
My wife stumbles through the back door,
trussed against the cold, snow in her hair.
Behind her mumbles oblivion,
its own engine, what the dying breathe.
I am glad to see her,
glad she is safe,
and tell her so.

Meg searches in the spice cabinet
for cumin. *What does it look like?*
Like curry, the gold dust in Indian food.
The recipe calls for a quarter of a teaspoon.
A half of a half, says Meg.
She is right in a way that matters
so we put the lid on the pot.
The soup will want two to three hours.
The black beans gurgle in protest
at their fusion with broth and the clear blood of olives.
I tell Meg to turn it down to simmer.
Simmer is as low as you can get.
Simmer is what they do,
the Tibetan monks from Drepung Loesling,
when they empty themselves
and hum upon what is gone.

My wife is a reindeer woman.
Now, after a snow nap,
she clacks in the kitchen
and will not wear shoes.
The sky clears to the west.
The squalls sleep just above us.

Simmer, little black brothers, loving, glum.

THE LADY OF THE LAKE READS FROM THE BOOK OF THE DEAD

The souls of the drowned
have long lingered over Vernor lake,
water visitors who cannot free
themselves from its grip.
At the moment of undoing,
the shucking of the body,
the new dead begin the crossing,
but water so resembles spirit
they cling to the lake,
its formlessness and clarity.

When the city of Olney drained
the lake down in 1995,
to repair the one hundred year old earthen dam,
drained the fifty three acres of water
down the spillway into Fox creek,
the indentured souls washed free
into the bottoms, riding the water slide
to the Embarras river, to the Wabash,
to the Ohio, to the Mississippi,
out into the Gulf of Mexico, its deep.
The last to leave was Vernice Summers
who had drowned herself a decade before,
walking off the end of the pier with her cane,
the black parachute of her skirts.
She wandered over the waters
till her husband Dutch came back for her,
taking her hands, the two of them tumbling
over the spillway, free.

The static in the wind has subsided.

The blue heron have returned.

WEARING THE WEDDING MASK

When Lu and I married four years ago, our friends the Bartles presented us with a Lady of Guadelupe, three feet high, a concrete statue in alabaster, the sorrowful mother both aroused and beatific, treading on the serpent, her heel pinning his bruised head to the earth. They found her at one of those roadside concrete statuary corrals. She was fenced in with deer, dwarfs, ducks, mushrooms, and countless Buddhas, the big bellied, laughing Ho-Tis and his Japanese sister, Kwan-yin, the other dutiful mother who pours her oil on the troubled waters. Al and Deborah loaded her in the trunk and brought her to the wedding. Whoever cast her decided to paint the corona, the spikes of light which emanate from her, a deep blue. She is surrounded and held by that.

My wife drives up in her old Mazda, named after the Persian god of light. I always know it is her because the auxiliary fan is locked on high. It sounds like a threshing machine. I cannot fix it. I will overcome it by including it, forgiving it for its high pitched, teeth knashing whine. Louder it gets, quieter I get. This doesn't work all the time. Lu carries in gladiolas, chicken, potatoes and shrimp. *What have you been doing?* she asks. I have been thinking how each tree is a mountain. I have been watching the winged lives at the feeder, the black capped chickadees, the nuthatches, a bedraggled cardinal, his plumage faded, a goldfinch. I have been drinking red wine from Australia, the old vines surrendering their bounty, the ruptured grape. I am learning to walk on stilts, made of the old growth, that first witness.

Ignorant of the Language, I Offer Five Translations of Characters Inscribed on an Ornamental Brass Box

The sparrow's sword is rusted
after the acid snow of winter.
He sharpens it on the whetstone
of this green hour.

The weather bleached wood of the trellis
is held upright by the tangled brown
fingers of the clematis vines.
Call it April's harp, its music
gathering into bloom.

From the mountain top, the levied
rice fields in the valley shine
in the day's last light. Scales
from a butchered golden carp.
A mother's tears hammered paper thin.

The Banyan tree of heaven grows
downside up. The climb toward graves,
mausoleum of cloud, tombstone stars.
The blind mole tunnels into the jet stream,
that underground river. His striving is done.

I am called Maria. This box belongs to me.
If you find it, keep it, though it will
never be yours. Whatever you hide
in it will be lost. My sari is the color
of bruised plums. I wash my black hair
in red wine. If you were to see me,
you would have to love me.

I Think I'll Take a Little Walk Downtown

At the Edwardsville tavern, whiskey, summer, jukebox,
big wheel keep on churnin, proud mary keep on burnin,
Candy Mudd, halter top, cut off, half moon jeans,
danced barefeet over to my table, Candy Mudd.
Oh sweet beer, sweet dirt,
mix me some Candy Mudd one more time.
Candy Mudd handed me a scrap of paper, danced away.
This, in a childish, penciled scrawl:
What is true no two men know.
What is gone is gone.

At Fisherman's wharf, San Francisco, thirty years ago,
I was sitting at a coffee shop, front table.
Outside, on a bench, a father, mother
and ten year old boy talked quietly,
a large window between us.
I watched in pantomime.
The father stood up and walked down the street.
The mother spoke to the child, her hand on his arm.
The boy mouthed the word *no*,
hung his head and sobbed.
They stumbled away, her arm around his small shoulders.
I am still listening
for what she might have said, that knife.

When the neighbors moved out next door,
the pissed off, flat top woman who clerked
at the auto parts store and cursed her dogs,
the stone faced husband who sunned himself
in his backyard chaise lounge underwear,
porn magazines, beer, when they moved,
they left behind a ten foot curbside mound of trash,
crowned by dozens of thawing packages of frozen meat.
They hadn't paid the trash bill.
It was there for weeks till the city hauled it away,
a mortal, festering goodbye
to the neighborhood, a betcha can't climb
this Himalaya.

When my father left, he was three coffee cans

of bone and ash, strewn from the bridge
into the Embarras river, first the bone pellets
plinking into the muddy water, then the settling
of the heavier ash. A lighter dust hung
over the river for a long while, like the smoke
from fireworks, before coming apart
and joining the darkness.

If You Cannot Find the Truth Right Where You Are, Where Do You Expect to Find It?
—Dogen

Find it in the letter the mailman refused
to deliver. Go chase him down the sidewalk.
Take back what belongs to you.

Find it in the Goodwill, the dead man's suits
without shoulders, hung in a row.
Check the left breast pocket. Wear that one home.

Find it in the grocery, underneath the cart
where you stow the potatoes and the cat litter.
Sometimes the truth is low down.

Find it on your backstep, the one black shoe
heavy as a stone, the laces in a hard,
hard knot.

Find it in yesterday's half frozen cup
of muddy coffee you left on the porch rail.
Drink it down. Shoulder the morning.
A clear, blind river runs beneath your feet.

Find it in your own breath,
the windhorse that carries you
across this plain, toward the mountains.

If you cannot find the truth where you live,
where does it live, this truth you live for?

More rain. Mom and I drive down to the old home place, the Totten farmland, S.E. of Olney. The creeks are out, chocolate roil through the culverts, across the roads. We are turned back three times by high water. Near the Weesner place, I find a last remaining stand of wild asparagus that has somehow survived the herbicides, the same patch Mom and Dad cut from in the late 1930's. Dad pointed it out to me years ago. I gathered asparagus here in the 1970's. Thumb thick tender shoots, spring bounty, Illinois bamboo funk you can smell in your piss an hour later. The ditch is full of water. We can't get across it to the asparagus today. It won't go away. We will. No one will cut our hair a hundred years from now.

Mom won't let me drive through the six inches of water covering the road, tells me if I try it, she'll get out of the car. She remembers a time when she was a child, her older brother Oscar drove through the flooded Higginswitch, a mile east of here. Just past Shields school, the car stalled, the muddy current running over the floorboards. The two of them huddled in the car till daybreak, the car rocking in the flood, Mom certain it would tumble away and drown them. At first light, a neighboring farmer found them and pulled the car to safety with a tractor. Mom says the water over the road makes her feel funny in the pit of her stomach. We don't cross.

At the Dollar store, mom wants to buy flowers for the graves in her head, my brother Michael, her brother Oscar, her parents Chester and Blanche Totten. She sorts through the ten dollar wire frame bouquets, plastic roses and ferns. She prefers real flowers but says they don't last. I find a box of plain wooden crosses with a single plastic rose at the center nail. I offer one of these to Mom. She chooses four. Blue. Yellow. Maroon. Purple. The fourth color isn't right. She buys it anyway.

At Haven Hill cemetery, Mom can't decide which rose cross should be planted at each grave, and, though it has begun to rain again, the earth is as hard as a pool table. We can't get the pointed end of the first cross driven into the ground. I search for a hammer, under the seats, in the trunk. We'll come back tomorrow.

Later that week, on the way back to Ohio, I stop at the Yaeger bridge, east of Saint Marie, where I scattered my father's ashes five years ago. I've picked an iris from our yard, white bearded with a tangerine heart. I seal it in a quart mason jar and drop it from the bridge, twenty feet below into the current. The Embarras river will crest Friday, nine feet above flood stage. In the flower jar this note. *Daniel Wayne Ragain, 1916-1990. Whoever finds this, say my name.*

FITTING THE PIECES
—for Jim McCarthy

The painter is nearly done scraping the house.
The old trim steals his time, its blister and warp,
the wood cracking along the grain.
Sears and Roebuck hauled in the lumber
eighty years ago, flat bed rail cars
along the Cuyahoga river into Kent.
The mid October jet stream is bending.
I don't want him warming gallons
of paint on my kitchen stove.

My wife bought me four birthday
rose bushes, thick caned premium
two year olds, potted in five
gallon buckets, names round their necks,
lined up on the back porch, candles on my dirt cake.
We dream an arbor buckling,
an orchard of bloom outliving us both.
We dug one hole, before the rains,
east of the house, dull shovel, small crater.

No one suspects the days to be gods.
A banner of yellow paper
taped to my door.
This day is named for Saturn, his leaden watch,
his slow turn in darkness,
his breath in the trees, tearing gold,
killing the hours.

You once told me renunciation
is nothing more than understanding
that things, in accord with their nature,
must go away. No one knows where away is.
Perhaps it is not far, in a measure we cannot count.

I see the way I am
but there is another life inside,
as shapeless as water,
mothered from a cold spring
of pure sadness.
This is the life we share.

The Miracle of the Northern Lights

Five years ago, grapefruit size cancers were climbing
Billy's backbone, tumors threading his ribcage
as if he were a trellis to be overrun.
When he could no longer walk, Billy rolled around Kent
in his wheelchair, one end of town to the other,
sometimes all night, singing and weeping,
as if to wear out the cancers.
He renounced the chemo, its slow burn,
pulled the plug and holed up in his trailer.

A couple of years later, he walked up to me
in the Brady cafe, hugged me hard and said
God bless you, brother. He meant it,
calling down God's blessing on me where I stood.
I'm alive because I gave it all to Jesus.
No doubt what it was. In that moment
I believed in him, in Jesus,
the cavalcade of miracles, the stigmata,
the dancing bones of the saints, the lady of Guadalupe.
Billy's eyes crackled with sweet love from nowhere.

Today, I found Billy in the Hills department store
parking lot, pushing a flotilla of twenty or so
carts to the front door, all wedged inside one another,
his knees bent for leverage.
His orange vest marked him as an employee,
not a homeless shopping cart pilgrim.
After he had wrangled the herd of carts
through the sliding doors, he came back
for a maverick at the lot's far corner.
I drove up to him and offered my hand.
Billy was still happy, that borealis light in his eyes,
still sunkissed by his blessing.
When I told him I was driving to Oregon
to visit my son, Billy's eyes filled with rivers,
the Rouge, the Willamette, the Columbia,
with mountains, the Cascades, the Sawtooth.
Billy had lived there for a year,
in a national forest consorting with bears,
eating peeled bark, boiling snow.

Would I say hello to the rivers,
to the mountains for him.
We shook hands. He blessed me again.
You have to have it to give it.
It is the brush of unseen lips.
It is a pillar of fire.

Billy bends to his work, this shepherd of the carts.
Hopeful beanstalk to heaven carts.
Silver basket mantra carts.
Beaded rosary, hail mary mother of grace carts.
Devil go back to hell carts, satan you can't catch me carts.
Everything is holy carts, bind the wounds of the children carts.
Cross the river styx carts, final clearance red tag carts.
Fly with me to heaven carts, storewide savings moonlight madness carts.
Brother take a load off and put it right on me carts.
The body is more than raiment carts.
The life is more than meal carts.
Don't leave your soul unattended carts.
Love outlives death carts, take me into your chest
like burning coals carts, whirling dervish be still carts.
You don't need a machine to breathe carts.

Death cannot find a seat on Billy's silver train
across this desert of asphalt.
Sweet Billy, blessed by his blessing.
Billy, let me ride.

Jimmie The Vincennes Flyer (1977) 20pp. Tom Beckett, editor. Viscerally Press. *Viscerally Six*. Chapbook $1, 7 by 8.5 in. Edition of 100. Saddle stapled, white 70lb. cover, 50lb interior paper. Illustrated by Kenny Muenzenmayer. This chapbook consists of six poems with three interior illustrations.

The Olney Dreadnot Book (1979) 64pp. Kenny Muenzenmayer, editor. Shelly's Press. Perfect Bound $6, 6.5 by 10 in. Edition of 400, Letterpress, three colors (maroon, blue, and black) imprinted on light grey 80lb cover. Four color (maroon, blue, red, and black) letter press frontpage. Printed on 60lb cream colored paper with interior poems printed in maroon, section dividers in blue, and illustrations in black ink. Illustrated by Larry Marcell (10 illustrations and cover). One illustration by Kenny Muenzenmayer. Ragain's first full length book. Shelly's Press was an Ohio based poets co-operative which published a national literary journal as well as full length books, chapbooks, and broadsides, 1974-1981. 2nd printing. 1998 Wrappers $8, 6.5 by 10 in. Edition of 50. Blue library vinyl reinforced spine with name of book and author on maroon tape.

7 Poems (1980) 10pp. Bill Polak, editor. PullPress. Chapbook N.P., 5.5 by 8.5 in.Edition of 100, Black thread sewn binding, 60lb sunflower yellow cover, light blue tip in, 50lb white pages.

Northfield Thistledown Making Book (1981) 20pp. Tout Press. Chapbook $3, 7 by 8.5 in. Edition of 200, Letterpress, two color (red and black) cover imprinted on light brown 80lb paper. Black thread sewn binding, dark brown 80lb tip in. Three color (black, red, maize yellow) letter press frontpage. Printed on 60lb ivory paper, three interior charts printed in red ink. This is a split chapbook, five poems are by Virgil Smith, six poems are by Maj Ragain. The final book printed using Shelly's Press.

Father Sky (1984) Kenny Muenzenmayer, editor. 8pp. Three Hawk Press. Wrappers $2, 7 by 8.5 in. Edition of 100, Saddle stapled, periwinkle blue cover, navy blue tip in. 60lb Classic Leaf white paper. Illustrated by Kenny Muenzenmayer. This chapbook consists of two poems and two interior illustrations.

Gail Ray's Drowning in Olney Poem (1987) Virgil Smith, editor. 8pp. Catcher Press. $2, 6.5 by 8.5 in. Edition of 100, Saddle Stapled, light blue 80lb cover, cream 50lb paper. 2nd edition of 20 copies. 50lb white or yellow cover, light blue 50lb interior paper. Illustrated by Ruth Joy. This chapbook consists of one poem and four interior illustrations.

A Little Bastard Book for Buddha (1987) 24pp. Ostowegowa Press. Wrappers $2, 4.5 by 5.5 in. Edition of 100, Saddle stapled chapbook on 60lb white cover with 2.5 inch folded in flaps. The definition for Ostowegowa is printed sideways in black on the rear flap. Black tip in. Interior printed on 24lb white paper. Thirteen poems.

Fresh Oil, Loose Gravel (1996) 123pp. Burning Press. Wrappers $10, 6 by 9 in. Edition of 1000. Perfect bound. Cover is a 12 pt laminated stock without inner lamination, light brown color, with cover and two interior illustrations by Larry Marcell. Ragain's second full length book. Includes uncredited poems from *Jimmie The Vincennes Flyer*, and *A Little Bastard Book for Buddha*.

Burley One Dark Sucker Fired **(1998)**. 78pp. Bottom Dog Press. Wrappers $9.95. 6 by 9 in. Edition of 800, Perfect bound. Cover is printed on 12 pt C1S laminated stock, light blue color, with illustration of log cabin by Sheila Felton. Ragain's third full length book. Includes uncredited poems from *A Little Bastard Book for Buddha*.

Twist The Axe **(2000)** 134pp. Author printed edition. Not sold. Edition of 50. 6.25 by 9 in. Velobound. 80lb off white marble finish cover, cover illustration by Larry Marcell. Includes various horse racing newspaper articles not in final version.

Twist The Axe **(2001)** 164pp. Bottom Dog Press. Boards $30. Edition of 75. Signed w/silver gelatin print of Jim Lang's back cover photo. Wrappers $10.95. 6 by 9 in. Edition of 925. Book design by Daniel Schmidt. Cover photos by Jim Lang. Three poems in this version are not in the original. All are horseracing poems, some are from *Northfield Thistledown Making Book, A Little Bastard Book for Buddha, Fresh Oil, Loose Gravel,* and *Burley One Dark Sucker Fired.*

Vision to Verse/Verse to Vision: A Visual and Poetic Dialogue (2004) 24pp. Verde Gallery. Wrappers $8. 5.5 by 7.75 in. Edition of 1000. Saddle stapled. Full color cover and interior. Forward by William Tucker. Consists of 12 poems by Ragain and 12 paintings by Jessica Damen. Created as a program for their show held from June 15th to September 4th 2004. A collaborative chapbook with 9 responses by Ragain to Damen's art and three paintings created by Damen in response to Ragain's poems.

Maj Ragain was born on a Saturday morning, September 15, 1940, in Olney, a small farming community in southeastern Illinois. Father, a carpenter; mother, a homemaker. The poem, a thing made of language on hand, in and by hand. Wood, food, cloth, paper, that long tradition. Raised on Vernor lake, north of Olney, marriage of heaven and water, fishing the skylights. Education, the paved road out of town. Phd, Kent State University, 1990. Poetry, that dirt road winding back home, corn tassel, fencerows, the last light fading in the top branches of a century oak. Poetry, that slip knot, bridging solitude and community, a way to offer one's longings to the world. Maj has taught at Kent State University in Ohio, off and on, since 1969. For twenty years, through 2002, he hosted the open poetry readings at the Brady Café in Kent and presently at the North Water Street Gallery, open readings, breath lifting words from the page, a conversation still unfolding. A wife: LuAnn Csernotta. Two children: Sean Kelly and Megan Ryan. **A Hungry Ghost Surrenders His Tackle Box** is Maj's fifth collection of poems. He travels widely in Kent and ties his small boat to the back porch railing, 322 East Grant Street.